"With upwards of 50 percent of the workforce now 'agile' or temporary, organizations should take heed of Younger and Smallwood's words. As the world of work evolves and productivity pressures create leaner and leaner organizations, leading companies will have to consider how they create and optimize a compelling value proposition for the networks of resources involved in delivering their success. *Agile Talent* provides a valuable collection of insights, tools, and cases on which assets an organization needs to own, which ones it can rent, and which ones it merely needs to access. It represents a whole new way for organizations to work across their value chain and optimize the performance of the people who work for (and with) them to reach new levels of productivity."

　—TODD M. WARNER, former VP, Learning, BHP Billiton, and Founder, Like Minds Advisory

"Younger and Smallwood demonstrate a nuanced mastery of how to manage a modern business and make it more competitive by managing agile talent and cloud resources. This book presents a clear and effective description of how all businesses need to function in the future—or be left behind."

　—OMAR KADER, Chairman and CEO, Paltech

"This book is relevant, practical, and immediately applicable to anyone reading it, whether you are a CEO, a chief HR officer, a leader at any level in a company, or a shareholder looking for innovative ways companies are gaining competitive advantage in the marketplace. Building on their extensive experiences, research, client engagements, and insights, Jon Younger and Norm Smallwood articulate, in simple yet powerful ways, key trends that will significantly affect the way work gets done and ultimately how value gets created for shareholders. The issues, opportunities, and solutions raised in *Agile Talent* will enable me, an HR leader for a *Fortune* 500 company, to be a more effective steward of our talent, both internal and external."

—SUSAN J. SCHMITT, Senior Vice President, Human Resources, Rockwell Automation

"Younger and Smallwood's idea of agile talent and its deployment, in its various forms, is very powerful. At Driscoll's, it has allowed us to implement an approach that I refer to as '*virtual vertical integration*,' in which organizations can benefit from vertical integration but not suffer from the curse of multiple focus areas leading to mediocrity. It allows for specialization and entrepreneurial spirit to flourish but to be coordinated in a way that provides the benefits of vertical integration. This book helps advance that type of thinking."

—KEVIN MURPHY, CEO, Driscoll's

"In *Agile Talent*, Younger and Smallwood take a practice that happens routinely in every size and type of organization—contracting outside expertise. They challenge every reader to break free from our typical narrow and situational tactics and instead think strategically and holistically about how to approach external staffing."

—SHELLEY SEIFERT, Chief Administrative Officer, First Bank

"As HR professionals, our challenge often is to deliver a roadmap the business will want to follow and whose return on investment will be acceptable. But spending the budget to achieve the deliverables in human capital planning can sometimes be an obstacle. *Agile Talent* provides a rarely found treasure trove of experiences and practical solutions to outline the advantages of building capability with cost-effective methodology. It shows how to create an agile workforce that meets an organization's particular needs."

—KATHLEEN WILSON-THOMPSON, Executive Vice President and Global Chief Human Resources Officer, Walgreens Boots Alliance

"*Agile Talent* answers the question, 'How do we get the full benefit of having the best people where and when we need them—even though they're not on our payroll?' This book provides a roadmap for navigating to new and powerful workforce relationships."

—**KIRK AUBRY**, President and CEO, Savage

"Talent is the number one global business challenge, yet talent strategies are uninspired and largely conform to past practice. With this book, Jon Younger and Norm Smallwood outline a new approach—agile talent. They give us a solid strategic and practical roadmap on how this new approach to resourcing can provide real competitive advantage. A true example of workplace innovation. Recommended!"

—**EVEN BOLSTAD**, Executive Director, HR Norge

"The thinking provided by Younger and Smallwood in *Agile Talent* is highly relevant for every executive who wants to grow and increase their chances of success by providing strategic alignment and motivation among key stakeholders, including the ability to attract and nurture talents and skills—whether they are external or internal. *Agile Talent* provides a framework to reinvent strategic thinking and leadership to respond to the rapid market changes and new customer demands we're all likely to continue to experience."

—**DANIEL HUMMEL**, CEO and Managing Director, Falck Global Assistance

AGILE
TALENT

AGILE
TALENT

HOW TO SOURCE AND MANAGE
OUTSIDE EXPERTS

JON YOUNGER ◆ NORM SMALLWOOD

HARVARD BUSINESS REVIEW PRESS

BOSTON, MASSACHUSETTS

Printed in the United States of America

10 9 8 7 6 5 4 3 2 1

The web addresses referenced in this book were live and correct at the time of the book's publication but may be subject to change.

Younger, Jon, author.
    Agile talent: how to source and manage outside experts/Jon Younger, Norm Smallwood.
        pages   cm
    Includes bibliographical references and index
    ISBN: 978-1-62527-763-3 (alk. paper)
    1. Personnel management.   2. Consultants.   3. Human capital–Management.
    4. Contracting out.   I. Smallwood, W. Norman, author.   II. Title.
    HF5549.Y635 2016
    658.4'6–dc23   2015033380

The paper used in this publication meets the requirements of the American National Standard for Permanence of Paper for Publications and Documents in Libraries and Archives Z39.48-1992.

ISBN: 9781625277633
eISBN: 9781625277640

Contents

Foreword

In this valuable and forward-thinking book, Jon Younger and Norm Smallwood present a clear and cohesive roadmap for attracting, engaging, partnering with, and productively leading the work of external experts—what they've named "agile talent."

Organizations are relying more and more on experts sourced from a growing global talent network. Whatever they're called in your organization—external staff, contingent workers, free agents, contractors, or "gigsters"—it's crucial to know how to manage and lead them.

Writing about knowledge workers in a 1999 article in *California Management Review*, Peter Drucker states, "The most important contribution management needs to make in the 21st century is . . . to increase the productivity of knowledge work and knowledge workers." It's difficult to lead expert workers, and even more so when they are agile talent. They don't need to be told what to do—in fact over managing them could lead to errors or misunderstandings. What agile talent needs to be effective are leaders who look beyond the work itself and think about the conditions their organizations must have in place for these experts to do their jobs well. Is there a robust system of orientation and onboarding? Are the big-picture goals of their work spelled out? Are they provided the required support and relationships with the internal staff with whom they must collaborate? Are they treated with respect and friendship or suspicion? Jon and Norm address these questions head on.

Agile talent's rise, as the authors observe, "is transforming and revolutionizing the traditional relationship between an organization and its workforce and is making new demands on managers and leaders." In order to harness this combination of expertise and technology, to access and use the global talent network, and to continue to survive and thrive, organizations and leaders must shift from focusing internally to positioning their organizations to build external partnerships.

This is not an easy task—one might even say it is monumental—but it is manageable with a little help from Jon and Norm. Their comprehensive framework and methodology, their in-depth exploration of what agile talent workers are seeking, both from their careers and from their employers and clients, is outstanding in itself. The chapters on attracting and welcoming agile talent into your organization and how you can best engage and collaborate with your external experts are wise and highly actionable.

I hope you enjoy this wonderful and important book and that you find it of great benefit as you lead in the new age of agile talent!

—Marshall Goldsmith, *Thinkers50* Top Ten Global Business Thinker and author of the *New York Times* and *Wall Street Journal* #1 bestseller, *Triggers: Creating Behavior That Lasts—Becoming the Person You Want to Be*

AGILE
TALENT

1

Achieving Competitive Advantage Through Agile Talent

Trends, Opportunities, and Challenges

Nearly all contemporary organizations are increasing their use of talent from the outside—by engaging individuals, teams, and even firms in non-traditional work relationships and alternate forms of employment—for strategic ends. Insurance companies Munich Re and AIG utilize external meteorological experts to better factor weather into the assessment of risk. Google and Intel rely on experts in social science and biomechanics to develop transformative products by better understanding how people think about and use technology. *The Times of India* works regularly with external advisers and educational institutions like the Indian School of Business (ISB) to develop the culture and executive skills its executives need to compete regionally and nationally. Huawei, the Chinese high technology giant, benefits from global consulting firms as it builds its powerful global franchise. McKesson, the US-based pharmaceutical and health-care giant, has found external expertise an increasingly strategic extension of its resources in areas such as business strategy and logistics support. And at the same time, McKesson provides external expertise to health-care providers in health-care-related information technology (IT), physician practice management, and home care and hospice advisory services.

Companies like Google, Huawei, and McKesson are gaining advantage through a more strategic use of external expertise made possible by technology and the globalization of talent. Managers in these companies understand that agile, fast, and lean strategies require that they think in new ways about accessing and leveraging key strategic talent and filling critical gaps in strategic capabilities. We call this increased use of external resources, for strategic purposes, a shift to *agile talent*. And we've coined *cloud resourcing* to describe how companies utilize agile talent: through technology-enabled access to a global talent network. Agile talent, powered by cloud resourcing, offers companies a greater range of skills—especially those deemed strategic—on a more cost-efficient basis than is available from traditional models of employment.

And it isn't just companies making the shift—half of the UK government budget will go to non-civil-service professionals and organizations providing services to Great Britain. Nor is this shift confined to large companies—Intuit, forecasting big changes ahead in how small businesses will be staffed in the future, predicts that the shift to a contingent workforce (freelancers, contractors, part-timers, and other individuals who are moving away from more traditional employment relationships) will change how small businesses are run (see the sidebar "The Size of the Agile-Talent Workforce").

Agile talent is everywhere. Geographic and industry differences are irrelevant. The shift from cradle-to-grave employment to a more flexible and agile workforce is as bullish in Singapore as it is in Silicon Valley, and as evident at Rosneft, a Russian oil company, as it is at

THE SIZE OF THE AGILE-TALENT WORKFORCE

Studies of the global agile-talent community vary in their estimates of the size of the population. In 2013, Accenture suggested that 20 to 30 percent of the total workforce falls outside the organization's traditional full-time, permanent employment relationship. More recently, Deloitte estimated that 30 to 40 percent of corporate FTEs are supplied by external resources. The UK government reported that over 50 percent of the national budget was spent on external resources. And in a particularly interesting study, Freelancers Union, a US-based organization, reported that a quarter of the US workforce were project-based independents (what we call *gigsters*) working for more than one organization.[1]

All of these studies vary somewhat in their definition of the population, and some studies include certain outsourcing activities that we would not include in our definition of agile talent. But regardless of differences in magnitude, it is clear that the agile-talent movement is large and appears to be growing significantly.

Chevron and British Petroleum. And although both corporate and public sector executives want to get the most value possible from external strategic talent, their organizations are not set up for it. Therein lies the dilemma, and the purpose of this book.

Trends

Over the past several years, as we've worked with a wide range of leading organizations and governments around the world, teaching, consulting, and conducting research, we've noticed a number of important and powerful developments.[2]

First, as competition accelerates and as innovators disrupt indus-tries and markets, the need for "expertise on tap" continues to expand. Organizations are thus increasingly reliant on a widening range of functional external experts to acquire and master the capabilities needed to perform and grow. And not only are organizations likely to need new or increased capabilities, they need them sooner; the required speed of change has vastly accelerated. Deloitte, for example, reported that just over half the companies it surveyed say their need for "contingent workers" will continue to increase over the next three to five years (figure 1-1).[3]

Second, much of this external talent is composed of highly trained expertise. Consider Bain Capital. This $70 billion buyout firm has its origins in the strategy consulting industry made famous by its found-ing CEO and former US presidential candidate, Mitt Romney. The old model of private equity connected portfolio companies with generalist partners or associates. But times have changed, and firms like Bain attract portfolio companies by offering a range of external resources—the private-equity industry calls them *operating partners*—with the expertise to improve the performance of these companies. Operating

FIGURE 1-1

Respondents' plans for use of external talent

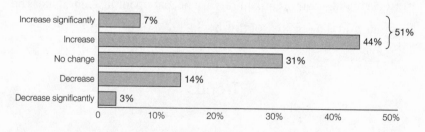

Source: Lisa Disselkamp, Werner Nieuwoudt, and David Parent, "Workforce on demand," Deloitte University Press, February 27, 2015, http://dupress.com/articles/on-demand-workforce-human-capital-trends-2015/.

Note: Percentages do not total 100 percent due to rounding.

partners offer skills in nontraditional areas like supply-chain management, human resources, sustainability, digital marketing, and customer service. As Pat Hedley, a former managing director of Atlantic Capital, put it, "Private equity firms are the 'cloud resource' for the businesses in their orbit."[4]

Campbell's similarly looks to highly trained external expertise for help. The US food company bombed when it first entered the Chinese market, thinking its traditional formula for success—open the can, heat, and eat—would play as well in China as in the United States. But it didn't; Campbell's strategy didn't appreciate the deep pride Chinese homemakers took in their soup making. But by tapping the experience of anthropologists, Campbell's relaunched soups, providing rich base broths that enabled Chinese homemakers to make homemade-like soups by adding their own meats and vegetables.

Third, this technical expertise is more accessible globally, the result of greater educational and economic opportunity. More countries are producing more PhDs in more technical and professional fields. Data from the journal *Nature* shows this rise clearly (figure 1-2).[5] While reasonable observers may disagree on the rigor of technical preparation

FIGURE 1-2

Increased availability of experts: average annual growth of doctoral degrees across all disciplines, 1998–2006

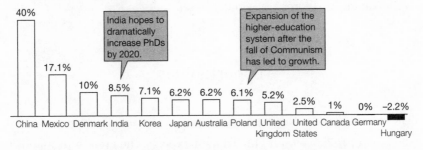

Source: Zhu Lui and Yong Geng, "Is China Producing Too Many PhDs?" *Nature,* June 2011.

across countries, there is no doubt that technical expertise is experiencing a global boom.

China produced 40 percent more students with scientific doctorates in the past decade. Mexico graduated 17 percent more PhDs. New technical fields are being created at a faster clip than ever before, the result of industry and technological pull. For example, bio-nanotechnology is a recently created discipline that unites and integrates the fields of physics and synthetic biology. It has extraordinary opportunity for growth and contribution, yet only in the past few years has it become a distinct field of applied research.

Finally, both organizations and individual professionals are rethinking the idea of "careers." A growing number of businesses such as Zappos and LinkedIn have eschewed traditional employment relationships for new, flexible, and temporary arrangements that offer engaging work rather than full-time, permanent employment. Facebook has gone on record in saying that it is as interested in temporary employees as it is individuals with longer-term career interests. *Itinerants* is one term that social scientists use to describe these individuals, but it is not our favorite. Terms that are more descriptive, like *free agents*, *project junkies*, *tour-of-duty allies*, or *gigsters* (our favorite), better capture the trend and its vibe. But whatever this large and growing cohort is called, individuals who sojourn in organizations now represent as much as 20 to 40 percent of the workforce, as the sidebar "The Size of the Agile-Talent Workforce" previously noted.

Opportunities

These four trends—the expanding dependence on external resources, the greater reliance on highly trained experts, the greater availability of expertise in response to educational and economic opportunity, and the changing interests and expectations of the emerging workforce—add up to the big shift that we are calling *agile talent*. Agile talent is transforming and revolutionizing the traditional relationship between an organization and its workforce and is making new demands on managers and leaders. Innovative companies are leading the way, applying a broader palette of talent options and relying on more varied types of relationships. Leaders who embrace these changes and respond effectively to these challenges build more-agile organizations and ultimately deliver better results than their competitors. No wonder organizations are increasingly finding that external relationships enable greater flexibility.

Benefits to the Organization

Agile talent is powered by what we call *cloud resourcing*. The allusion to cloud computing is intentional; *cloud* is a synonym for distributed computing over a network and reflects the greater ability of organizations to increase speed and efficiency by running applications on many connected computers at the same time. Cloud resourcing reflects the ability of organizations to access a global talent network that offers a greater range of skills, on a more cost-efficient basis, than is available from traditional models of employment and that enjoys a far broader variety of resourcing arrangements. In our view, agile talent provides organizations with flexibility to establish capability, reduce fixed costs, and overcome strategic inertia created by a misalignment of capability and competitive challenge. In contrast to traditional outsourcing, companies embracing agile talent don't "hand over" an administrative or analytic function to be managed on behalf of the company. Instead, they embed external expertise in a much broader range of critical activity—from strategic advisory work to functional problem solving to full-time technical involvement on a contractual basis in new technological innovation. Our research (see the sidebar "Evidence on Which This Book Is Based") has shown that organizations are shifting to a workforce of agile talent, powered by cloud resourcing, for various reasons (table 1-1).

Furthermore, we have found that the increased reliance on external staff is meant to supplement, not replace, internal staff. As figure 1-3 indicates, executives clearly described external talent as supplemental.

We also asked why the use of externals was on the rise. The answers explicitly reinforce our view that cost, while important, is secondary to

TABLE 1-1

Key drivers and benefits of agile talent

Driver	Benefit
Expertise	External talent can provide companies with unique expertise— credibility, skill, and experience that are not currently available to the company internally.
Cost	Cost savings are often an objective sought through agile talent. Savings result when external talent is able to provide a more efficient solution than is available to the company, for example, through a less costly workforce or more-efficient work tools and methods.
Access to new technology	External partners are often sought for their more innovative or up-to-date technology. External talent may provide technology solutions that are unavailable to the company or would not make investment sense for the company.
Speed	Working with external agile talent enables a company to increase the speed at which the organization is able to bring expertise to opportunity. Rather than long waits to hire, it can deliver specialized skills immediately.
Market discipline	Seeking the assistance of external expertise can help an organization test the cost and value of a business opportunity without deep fixed investment in expertise.
Flexibility	The use of agile talent increases flexibility by providing additional means of gaining the expertise and experience required to take advantage of an opportunity, as well as exiting areas of talent and skill when it makes sense to focus elsewhere. External talent also provides functional flexibility by enabling organizations to deploy their critical resources where the need is greatest.

FIGURE 1-3

Agile talent is a supplement, not a replacement, for internal staff

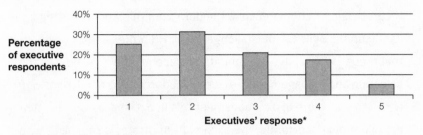

Source: RBL Group survey (2013).

*Responses from the RBL pilot survey of 200 executives answering the question "Are your external resources generally supplementing your internal staff or replacing it?" on a scale of 1 to 5, where 1 = supplementing internal staff, 3 = equally supplementing and replacing internal staff, and 5 = totally replacing internal staff.

EVIDENCE ON WHICH THIS BOOK IS BASED

While a good deal of research has looked at the general topics of exter-nal talent—the use of consultants, the rise of the "expert economy," and the increasing size of the freelance population in the United States and elsewhere, no recent studies have specifically looked at how organiza-tions are set up to receive external resources and maximize the value and productivity of this outside work. Our data collection consisted of the survey results from two hundred executives. The executives, whose names were obtained from the RBL Group database, responded to a brief questionnaire. The data from this pilot study, while still preliminary, points out the need for organizations and executives to better align themselves to gain the full benefit of investments in external talent.

Reinforcing data on agile talent comes from RBL Group–sponsored research in two related areas. First, RBL Group is well known for col-laborating with the Ross School of Business, University of Michigan, to conduct the largest and most comprehensive ongoing global study of

HR professional competencies. The data from this work bears significantly on the agile talent challenge. While HR professionals point out that they typically have no mandate and spend little or no time on the selection and management of external resources, the need is growing for HR to play more of a management role in external as well as internal talent. As importantly, the alignment of strategic capability with organization and work design, and talent and performance management, is emerging as a key HR competency.[6]

A second related data source is RBL's leadership research, which incorporates the company's collaboration with Aon Corporation and *Fortune* magazine on the assessment of top companies for leaders and RBL's research on the leadership code.[7] Our data from this work is described later in this volume and points out the importance of a leader's role as a human capital developer responsible for anticipating and planning for the resources needed to compete and grow. In this area, agile talent is a key part of the organization's overall resourcing strategy. It is also the competency factor where leaders score lowest.

the ability to access new competitive capabilities required to perform and grow (table 1-2).

Benefits to the Individual

Lee Raymond, former chairman of Exxon Mobil, was known to say, "If a technology is important to us, we will own it." But those days are gone. Just as companies like Exxon Mobil are making increased use of external talent, the emerging workforce has indicated a growing preference for alternatives to permanent, full-time employment with a singular

TABLE 1-2

Top five reasons why organizations use agile talent

1	Leverage the increased availability of expertise
2	Reduce cost
3	Avoid adding to permanent headcount
4	Increase speed of getting things done
5	Challenge organization's thinking and assumptions with outside ideas

Source: RBL Group survey (2013).

employer. Libby Sartain, former HR head of Southwest Airlines and Yahoo, describes millennials as adopting a "gig" economy. As she put it, high-performing and talented technical professionals are often less interested in a conventional career than they are in being guns for hire, looking for the next cool project or innovative business.

Reid Hoffman, cofounder of LinkedIn, describes a similar logic; he describes the focus on interesting work, rather than permanent employment, as "tours of duty."[8] Jamie Gutfriend of the Intelligence Group (a division of Creative Artists Agency) describes the current crop of young professionals as "'venture consumers,' looking for opportunities to invest in a place where they can make a difference, preferably in a place that itself makes a difference."[9]

The win-win is obvious. For individuals, cloud resourcing provides new career options. For organization leaders, it is a fast and powerful response to the need for agile talent. For example, in the United States, it is not easy to attract top investment managers out of New York City, London, or Hong Kong and persuade them to move to a regional bank in the US Midwest. But an organization can easily arrange for investment management expertise to provide service to a Midwest bank's customers through "open architecture." The greater availability of all forms of expertise provides a huge opening for many organizations to access skills that they could not otherwise attract or afford. The ability to disconnect work from time and place creates unique opportunity. For example, Cisco executives talk about the impact of technology in creating the "business mobility" generation of knowledge work.[10] Of all respondents in an internal Cisco survey, 60 percent said they would work more from home in the future. Some 40 percent believed mobility enables them to have greater choice over how, when, and where they work.

The organization that can disconnect from traditional workplace limitations has the advantage of attracting and utilizing external experts who are distributed widely but able to work with the organization remotely through new communications technology. Consider Princeton University's $17 billion endowment fund, which is essentially a large hedge fund. In fact, if it were ranked among hedge funds, it would be among the top twenty-five largest hedge funds in the world. Managing that large an endowment requires the ability for fund professionals to work closely with external investment managers in a wide variety of specialties. Princeton may be located in suburban New Jersey, but its advisers are as globally dispersed as its investments are. Unsurprisingly, the head of Princeton's endowment fund earns significantly more than the university's president does.

Challenges

So what are the challenges? As more and more companies look to the cloud to access and leverage agile talent, they are increasingly bumping up against several big issues.

Relationship Management

When managing outside talent, managers simply have a harder time than we might expect. Full stop. In a recent survey, 50 percent of IT heads reported frustrations with IT service partners, claiming that promises of high touch and attention were often inconsistent with the reality once contracts were signed. Relationship management challenges are greater still when differences in time zone or culture create added barriers. And all too often, the foundation for sustained and successful partnership is not built well enough. Goals are unrealistic. Flexibility is not as great as promised. Costs increase as services are added or improved. And experts move from one company to another, leaving skill gaps. Not surprisingly, organizations struggle to maintain relationships between themselves and their external resources. For example, 25 percent of outsourcing relationships fail within two years, and 50 percent fail within five years. In the marketing field, a recent study found that average client-agency relationship tenure dropped from over five years in 1997 to less than three years today. The study points out several factors as responsible, but emphasizes the "failed relationship," which is based on client and external partner turnover, lack of understanding of the client's business, or understaffed and inexperienced external resources.[11]

Why do these relationships fail? One of the problems is decision making. Too often, purchasing departments manage the selection while operating managers—not involved in selection by fiat—are expected to make the relationship work. This arrangement is often complicated by inconsistent decision criteria: purchasing wants the lowest price and a fixed cost, whereas the business or operation wants the best resource, a good cultural fit, and enough flexibility in the contract to allow for changes in scope or strategy. But there are also extrinsic factors that complicate the relationship. For example, tax rules in the United States and other countries are biased toward full-time employment relationships. As a result, many organizations keep external resources at arm's length to avoid potential legal problems and fines.

Internal-External Competition

External talent can be a tremendous benefit to organizations, but may also be threatening to internal managers and internal technical professionals, especially agile talent that offers strategic benefits, is highly trained, and possess capability that internals don't. Gallup reports a general erosion of employee engagement.[12] Employees may feel threatened when their organizations use external resources. Long-term employees may wonder if externals have the organization's best interests at heart, and cultural clashes are a potential problem.

External resources are often part of the problem. For example, a consultant colleague of ours was asked by a company's new CEO to "help the head of HR and her team to increase the contribution of HR to the business." This chief HR officer was administratively competent but not strategically oriented. Rather than appreciate the delicacy of the HR head's position ("Can the HR head and I develop an effective relationship?"), the consultant jumped right into discussions with executive team members on the needs for change in HR. Instead of helping the HR head, our colleague inadvertently worsened the situation by spotlighting the competency gap. The lesson was clear: internals and externals must work together rather than independently (or competitively).

Clash of Expectations

Just as internal people might feel threatened by external talent, smart externals may believe that the organizations for which they work are too slow, too bureaucratic, and too complex. Similarly, organizations view externals as clueless about the business and unwilling or unable to have a deep understanding of the organization's issues. These attitudes are a setup up for failure.

TABLE 1-3

Top complaints from internal executives and external talent about the client-agency relationship

Internal executive concerns about external talent	External talent complaints
• It is difficult to find external talent that matches our culture.	• Organization is too slow in making decisions.
• External talent doesn't know us or our business well enough to contribute.	• Organization is too complex and heavy-handed.
• External talent is too abstract in its approach.	• Internal staff don't work hard enough.
• External talent lacks commitment to our organization.	• It's difficult to access senior leaders.
• External talent often seems to be reading from a script or operating a "program" rather than trying to understand our unique problems and address them appropriately.	• Leader buy-in and support for externally resourced projects are often weak or inconsistent.

Source: RBL Group Survey (2013).

To get a better feel for these dynamics, the research pilot described in the sidebar "Evidence on Which This Book Is Based" also asked both internal executives and external talent to describe their experience. We asked the executives, "What are the two or three typical internal staff complaints you hear when you are working with external resources?" And we asked the external consultants, "What are two or three typical complaints you have about working with organizations?" The chief concerns each group had about the other are presented in table 1-3.

Failure to Deliver Results

A fourth challenge is the failure to deliver expected results. A recent McKinsey global survey found that just 26 percent of surveyed executives say that key change initiatives were successful at sustainably improving the organization.[13] Given that virtually all such projects deeply involve external resources, one aspect of the failure to meet expectations is no doubt rooted in how the organization selects, engages, and manages the performance of external resources and the quality of the internal-external partnership. An IBM study reported that only 40 percent of change projects met their schedule, budget, and quality goals—and that poor teamwork internally and with external colleagues was a major factor.[14] An Economist Intelligence Unit similarly found that 37 percent of business change projects utilizing external and internal staff failed to deliver benefits.[15] For the UK government, which relies critically on external resources, the chief of program and systems delivery at the Department for Work and Pensions reported to the *Guardian* that "only 30% of our projects and programs are successful."[16] And perhaps one of the more alarming statistics: a McKinsey study pointed out that almost 20 percent of large IT projects involving significant external resources go so badly they represent an existential threat to the organization.[17]

The Solution

Organizations are having these problems because, historically, organizations have treated externals as "separate, and not equal." Most managers would never dream of treating externals like internals. External agile talent is hired for expediency, for the short term, to fill a specific need. But as companies depend more on this agile talent for fulfilling strategic capabilities, that mind-set won't cut it anymore. "Separate, and not equal" is precisely what is causing the problems just outlined.

In this book, we argue that managers need to fundamentally change how they think about this population of talent and that they should treat externals like internals: separate and equal. We have found that the organizations that get the most from agile talent—and conquer the four big problems described above—use the most effective managerial techniques in engaging, motivating, and building teams with internal staff. Like full-time employees, external resources want to do meaningful work; grow in competence and opportunity; be respected, trusted, and engaged; be treated as a part of the team; receive ongoing communication about the issues that bear on their work; and feel rewarded fairly and recognized for their contribution and effort. Too often, they feel, instead, merely tolerated or treated as suspect by organization employees with whom they work. The feel unappreciated by management and powerless in dealing with the administrative bureaucracy of partner organizations.

In interviews with corporate leaders, we've noticed that many executives initially don't see the need to address how external resources are treated and managed. These business leaders are often ignorant about the details of how well their organizations are tuned—organizationally, administratively, and culturally—to create a positive and productive experience for agile talent. And in these discussions, most executives acknowledge the tendency to send mixed signals and the impact on the productivity and commitment of external resources. As one logistics company executive told us when we interviewed him:

> We know how to manage people in our company. And while we intellectually seek the benefits of a real partnership with external resources, the fact is that we generally treat them as a pair of hands and treat the relationship as essentially transactional— service for money. So we pay them a little late, tend not to think of involving them, et cetera. Interestingly, when we are working with *our* customers, it's just the reverse. We want to be treated as partners, while they treat us as the pairs of hands. We ought to learn from this. Our customers certainly get more from us when we feel that the relationship is a partnership. The same ought to go for our use of our externals resources!

The good news is that the answer to capturing greater value from your investment in external expertise is right in front of you: as the aforementioned logistics executive implies, all the management best practices that we already know to be effective for managing a traditional internal workforce need to be applied to this new and growing group of agile talent. But doing so involves some important twists. This book shows how to apply those twists.

How This Approach Is Different

A variety of books and other publications have pointed out the increasing reliance of organizations on external relationships and the potential benefit of agile talent. Yves Doz and Gary Hamel have articulately discussed "the art of creating value through partnering" in their description of how innovative companies are making greater use of alliances.[18] Kathryn Harrigan similarly describes best practices in joint venture relationships.[19] Martha Minow and Jody Freeman led an important conference at Harvard Law School to explain the practice and impact of outsourcing in the US federal government. The conference led to Minow and Freeman's book *Government by Contract: Outsourcing and American Democracy*.[20] And, of course, several recent reports in publications such as the *Economist*, *Fast Company*, and the *New York Times* have described how organizations are expanding their use of part-time, contract, and consulting resources as an efficient means of extending their workforce.[21]

But while this varied literature ably chronicles the general rise of new types of employment relationships, it is less articulate about creating the conditions for maximizing the engagement, performance, and contribution of agile talent. To date, there has been little focus on how to get the most from external talent—and how to manage teams that are increasingly composed of a mix of internal employees and people who fall outside the traditional employment relationship. This book will help fill these gaps. We believe that it provides an important missing link in discussions about the effective implementation of agile talent.

TEKsystems, a leading IT recruiter, reports that while contract work is increasingly preferred by young engineers and computer scientists over full-time employment, "consultants involved can feel they are treated more like a commodity than a talented individual."[22] As executives and external resources are both aware, and as the data we have collected makes clear, successfully deploying innovative talent strategies has important benefits, but only if the strategies are implemented correctly. And that means treating external resources in a different way than many have practiced.

Making Agile Talent Work

The effectiveness of agile talent is made or lost as a function of four critical factors, each representing an area of alignment between the organization and its external resources:

- **STRATEGIC ALIGNMENT:** Is the organization disciplined and rigorous in its identification of areas where agile talent and cloud resourcing are required or potentially beneficial? Has the organization identified the critical capabilities it needs to establish? Are relationships well thought-through? Is the organization effective at defining the role, relationship, and scope of initiatives addressed by consultants, advisers, or temporary technical experts? Does the work have the right level of sponsorship? Are timing, budget, and resourcing consistent with what is required for a successful outcome?

- **PERFORMANCE ALIGNMENT:** How well does the organization convert a plan or an initiative into well-defined, S.M.A.R.T. objectives and timelines? Are performance expectations clearly defined, established, and communicated? How often is performance assessed and feedback provided? What metrics are used, and are they reasonable? When performance problems arise, how promptly and effectively does the organization take the required action?

- **RELATIONSHIP ALIGNMENT:** How much is cultural fit as well as technical expertise considered in the choice of external talent? Are externals thrown into the task or given a solid orientation to the organization and the people with whom they will work? How are issues between internal staff and external resources resolved? Are externals engaged and treated with the consideration and respect that any individual would expect?

- **ADMINISTRATIVE ALIGNMENT:** Is the organization set up to work well with externals, or are they treated badly? Is the organization excessively bureaucratic in dealing with agile talent? Are the rules and procedures communicated appropriately? Are externals paid promptly? Is the orientation of the organization one that views external talent as a necessary evil or as welcome colleagues?

What This Book Will Do for You

In *Agile Talent*, we explore the requirements of this shift to agile external talent. We show what organizations and their leaders must do to gain sustainable value from their investments in external resources and service partners. More specifically, this book provides a roadmap for leaders who want to do a better job of managing, engaging, and increasing the productivity of external experts working for their organization. Companies that make the most of the agile-talent shift stand to gain both cost and competitive advantage. They gain flexibility and speed in their ability to change, and they enjoy exceptional access to outstanding external resources.

Making the best use of external talent requires thoughtful design and implementation in a variety of areas, from assessing your organization's needs, to onboarding external talent, to developing it. For executives, we provide a practical roadmap for strategic decisionmaking: what leaders need to do, and with whom, to take full advantage of cloud resourcing and agile talent (figure 1-4). We describe the specific steps: (1) defining the opportunity, (2) refining the specific talent resourcing strategy, (3) aligning the organization by choosing the right structure and arrangements to make cloud resourcing and agile talent work, and (4) leading the change.

For middle managers responsible for managing agile talent in their business unit or function, the book provides practical guidance on how to wisely choose among the talent options available from the cloud and how to create a work environment that encourages effective internal-external collaboration and high performance from external experts.

FIGURE 1-4

Making agile talent work

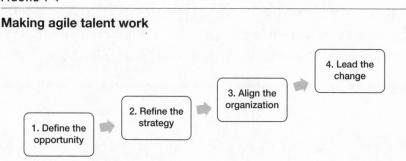

HOW WELL IS YOUR ORGANIZATION ALIGNED WITH AGILE TALENT?

Using the key alignment categories—strategic, performance, relationship, and administrative—test your organization by completing the four items in tool 1-1 as candidly as possible.

Your organization's effectiveness on these four factors will significantly determine how much benefit it will gain from agile talent in terms of speed, flexibility, and access to outside ideas and resources. We suggest that scores at the high end (6 or 7), if accurate, represent a strength that should be maintained and reinforced. This level of alignment provides a basis for real value creation through agile talent. Scores in the middle (between 3 and 5) should be a matter of interest: is this level of effectiveness consistent with your organization's current and future dependence on agile talent? Low scores (below 3) represent a likely need for improvement if your organization is to work effectively with external talent.

For a more rigorous and detailed diagnostic of your organization's readiness for agile talent, see the appendix, which provides an introduction to a diagnostic we call the *agile talent effectiveness quotient* (EQ). This brief survey provides a rigorous identification of how your organization can improve its reputation and effectiveness in attracting and working with top external resources. A more detailed version of the survey is available to readers without cost at the Agile Talent Collaborative website, agiletalentcollaborative.com. Learn more about the Agile Talent Collaborative in the appendix to this book.

TOOL 1-1

How agile-talent-aligned is your organization?

Using the key alignment categories described above, test your organization by completing the following four items as candidly as possible:

1. Rate your organization's strategic alignment with agile talent—how well linked to strategy, clear and realistic goals, the appropriate level of executive sponsorship, required support?

1	2	3	4	5	6	7
Consistently inadequate			Inconsistent (mix of both)			Consistently excellent

2. Rate your organization's performance alignment with agile talent—S.M.A.R.T. objectives, realistic time lines, clear performance metrics, disciplined and rigorous assessment, ongoing feedback?*

1	2	3	4	5	6	7
Consistently inadequate			Inconsistent (mix of both)			Consistently excellent

3. Rate your organization's relationship alignment with agile talent—the importance of cultural fit, good initial orientation, engagement and involvement, clear problem resolution processes?

1	2	3	4	5	6	7
Consistently inadequate			Inconsistent (mix of both)			Consistently excellent

4. Rate your organization's administrative alignment with agile talent—treatment of externals, non-bureaucratic procedures, prompt payment, fair problem resolution?

1	2	3	4	5	6	7
Consistently inadequate			Inconsistent (mix of both)			Consistently excellent

* S.M.A.R.T. is a well-known acronym describing the elements of a good objective: Specific, Measurable, Actionable, Realistic, Time-bound

The Logic of the Chapters

Chapters 2 and 3 focus on the first two elements of the roadmap—defining the opportunity and refining the specific resourcing strategy. We describe a comprehensive framework and methodology for doing so.

The next several chapters, beginning with chapter 4, focus on the third element of the framework—aligning the organization—and describe how effective leaders position their organization to build external talent partnerships. In chapter 4, we discuss what talented young people are looking for from a career and from their employers and clients. The chapter points out best practices in introducing agile talent into the organization and shows how smart leaders set up externals for success. Chapter 5 looks at how an effective organization designs work effectively for external experts and which competencies are the most important in ensuring the greatest contribution of external experts. Chapters 6 and 7 focus on how leading companies encourage partnership between internal and external colleagues and how to best motivate and engage external talent to maximize their contribution to your organization. These two chapters also explore the role and responsibility of leaders in building organizations that embrace new combinations of internal and external professionals as an agile workforce.

Chapters 8 and 9 focus on the last element of our framework—leading the change. Chapter 8 outlines change strategies for ensuring the effective management of agile talent, the implementation of cloud resourcing, and sustainability over time. Chapter 9 more generally considers the future of agile talent, cloud resourcing, and the organization.

2

Defining the Opportunity

Assessing How Agile Talent
Benefits Your Organization

The Abu Dhabi Investment Authority, or ADIA, is one of the world's largest sovereign wealth funds. ADIA is also an excellent example of an organization that is strategically and innovatively using agile talent. As of 2014, less than a third of ADIA's total workforce is Emirati. The remaining contributors to ADIA are external experts of every stripe, comprising a wide variety of nationalities. The total ADIA workforce includes full-time project consultants, advisers, expatriates on retainer, and numerous alliances and joint ventures focused on both investment performance and the development of the next generation of Emirati investment, trading, and functional support professionals.

From its early beginnings, ADIA senior management knew that success depended on a collaboration with outstanding external resources and partners. These relationships include financial experts working in Abu Dhabi, but also more innovative external partnerships. For example, ADIA "lends" young, high-potential Emirati professionals to firms such as Goldman Sachs for accelerated development and sends delegations to conferences and institutions to identify and return to ADIA with innovative business methods.

ADIA's decision to access external expertise is consistent with a broad range of organizations by taking advantage of the expertise outside its boundaries. As outlined earlier, access to expertise, increasing the speed of getting things done, and employing externals who challenge conventional thinking and assumptions were among the five top reasons for utilizing external experts.

The ADIA case offers a model for effectively utilizing agile talent: start by assessing the organization's strengths and needs, and then identify ways to utilize agile talent options to close what we might call the *organization capability gap*. Just as the London tube reminds riders to mind the gap, leaders and their human resource management team must clearly define the gap between the required capabilities they have and those they are lacking, if the organization is to powerfully implement its strategy. Closing the gap starts with talent but requires also aligning the organization, work systems, leadership style and skills, and culture.

Organization Capability

Throughout our work with many public- and private-sector organizations, we've found that a simple framework best supports an executive team's review of the company's strengths, its needs for improvement, and the role that agile talent might play. The starting point in defining both the benefits and the limitations is strategic organization capability.

Capability describes the critical strategic and operational skills an organization requires to achieve its goals. The terms *capability* and *competence* are often used interchangeably and, we think, incorrectly. Competence refers to individual expertise. Capability, by contrast, refers to the organizational level of expertise, for example, Toyota in efficiency, Google in innovation, or Shell in sustainability. It incorporates individual competence, but the essence of capability is how well the organization is set up, resourced, invested, and led to create powerful performance. Casey Stengel, the famous New York Yankees manager, once mentioned that a smart manager avoided tripping his players on their way out to the field, his point being that individual competence is a necessary but insufficient condition for sustained high performance. As one of us described along with Dave Ulrich in the *Harvard Business Review* article "Capitalizing on Capabilities," strategic capability unites individual and organizational effectiveness.[1]

In short, a firm creates organizational capability when it integrates technical and interpersonal competence with the firm's systems, structure, and ways of working. The intended result is an effective and focused organization where capabilities are aligned with its strategy. Organizational capability requires a well-defined and well-implemented system of organization, decision making, operations, relevant rewards, and ongoing executive leadership and behavioral reinforcement. As a comprehensive system of investment, expertise, and execution, capability is deeply rooted in a shared executive view of how the organization serves customers and challenges competitors.

ADIA and other organizations use agile talent to supplement key technical competencies that are crucial to organizational capability. For example, investment analytics are obviously an integral element of ADIA's effectiveness in producing significant profits and managing investment risk. Organizations that do not clearly identify and implement the capabilities required for success are less likely to sustainably achieve their goals and less able to target areas in which agile talent may offer advantages.

In "Capitalizing on Capabilities," Ulrich and Smallwood identified eleven typical areas of capability.[2] We invite you to assess your organization with a view to defining the critical capabilities on which your strategic performance depends, both now and in future. Table 2-1 describes some of these important organizational capabilities.

TABLE 2-1

Typical organizational capabilities

Capability	Description
Leadership	At all levels, developing leaders who generate confidence in the future
Strategic unity	Creating a shared cultural agenda and broad commitment and engagement around our strategy
Customer connectivity	Fostering strong and enduring relationships of trust with target customers
Corporate social responsibility	Establishing a strong reputation for sustainability, philanthropy, and employability in our industry and community
Shared mind-set	Ensuring that customers and employees have a consistent and positive experience of our firm's identity
Collaboration	Working together across boundaries to ensure leverage and efficiency
Learning	Generating, applying, and generalizing ideas with impact
Innovation	Creating new products, services, and ways of working that are commercially successful
Talent	Attracting, motivating, developing, and retaining talented and committed people
Speed	Making important changes rapidly
Efficiency	Reducing the costs of our business activities without hurting the core business
Accountability	Creating and enforcing standards that lead to high performance and execution
Partnership	Building effective partnerships and win-win working relationships with other companies in our industry
Risk	Assessing, evaluating, and managing risk

Capability Identification and Closing the Gap

In addition to its role as a wealth fund responsible for the future economic sustainability of the United Arab Emirates, the organization also has important obligations to the social goals of the country. The leadership of ADIA identified three strategic organizational capabilities as crucial to competitiveness:

- **PRUDENT INNOVATION**: balances the growth of the fund with a strong emphasis on managing risk

- **EFFECTIVE COLLABORATION**: produces strong returns by collaboration with and learning from colleagues and outside experts

- **DISCIPLINED EXECUTION**: ensures that goals and strategies are turned into actions

ADIA's choice of capabilities may be similar to the Norwegian or Malaysian sovereign wealth fund, but it need not be. Nor must it be similar to other large investment or pension funds. The choice of strategic organizational capability is unique to the organization and deeply rooted in its vision, strategy, culture, and the nature of its competition.

Must ADIA now invest equally and internally in these three capabilities? Certainly not. Instead, ADIA, or any other organization, must define specific performance drivers in each capability area and convert these to a *capability resourcing plan*. Doing so led ADIA to the decision, among others, to seek external partners or resources in various technical and commercial areas.

A good example is ADIA's decision to develop all of these areas through the accelerated development of leaders. The goal is an ambitious one; not only does it reflect the punishing demands on leaders of the global financial markets, but it is also about producing national leaders who will manage and guide the future of Abu Dhabi and the United Arab Emirates.

ADIA's multi-pronged strategy for leadership development includes several important moving parts:

- Leadership potential assessment

- Career planning

- Succession management

- Leadership academies

- Mentorship

- 360-degree feedback and coaching

- Secondment (temporary assignments to partner organizations) and other developmental assignments

- Educational opportunities

Some of these measures require internal expertise and management; succession management, for example, is an area for which ADIA leadership believes that full-time executive involvement is essential. In other areas, like programmatic leadership development through ADIA's leadership academies, it made sense for ADIA to develop relationships with key partners such as RBL Group, Harvard Business School, and INSEAD. Many organizations hire external leadership educators; what makes ADIA a particularly strong example of the agile-talent method is the strong, active sponsorship of executive management in supporting leadership development, the diligence with which the organization selects partners, the quality of collaboration in these long-term relationships, and the network of activities that make up a system of leadership development.

The specific steps in the analysis performed by ADIA executives follow this general approach:

1. *Identify* the capabilities required for success now and in the future.

2. *Define* the capability resourcing plan, including the assessment of current capability and needs for improvement.

3. *Clarify attractive opportunity areas* where external resources offer a time, cost, or knowledge advantage over alternative resourcing options.

4. *Proactively identify trade-offs*, risks, and other potential problems, and take necessary action.

Step 1: Identify the Capabilities Required for Success Now and in the Future

The outcome of this first step is obvious: organization leaders identify which capabilities are crucial to the strategy and goals of the organization. In some companies, the crucial capability is evident: at Nordstrom, it's customer connectivity; at Samsung, innovation; at Toyota, efficiency; and at Morgan Stanley, talent. In our experience, an outside-in approach is particularly helpful, starting with both the investor's and the customer's perspectives about which capabilities are best positioned to deliver what these stakeholders expect. A simple approach is to ask both key executives (internal) and key stakeholders (outside) three questions:

- In your experience, where do we now stand in these capability areas?

- What do you see as the top two or three organizational capabilities in which we must be best-in-class to meet your performance expectations now and in the future?

- How do you see our capability needs changing in the next three to five years to keep pace with industry, competitor, and customer developments?

Tool 2-1 is often helpful for comparing your own organization's capabilities with those of your competitors. We encourage leaders to set

TOOL 2-1

Identifying the capabilities required for success

In the first column, enter 1 to 5, where 1 = much worse than competition, 3 = on par with competition, 5 = much better than competition. Then select the top two or three capabilities that are required now and will be required in the future.

Capability	Rating versus competition	The top two or three capabilities that are required now	The top two or three capabilities that will be required in the future
Leadership			
Strategic unity			
Customer connectivity			
Corporate social responsibility			
Collaboration			
Learning			
Innovation			
Talent			
Speed			
Efficiency			
Accountability			
Partnership			
Risk			

a high bar when they compare their groups to competitors, and leaders collecting the ratings through interviews should challenge stakeholders to do likewise. For example, when asked to describe the company's innovative capability, sales leaders at Damco, the supply-chain division of A.P. Moller-Maersk, generally gave themselves high marks. However, when asked where Damco stood in relation to competitors, they rated themselves average.

Step 2: Design the Capability Resourcing Plan

The second step is to identify the key technical and functional skills that, together, constitute the capability. Think of organizational capability as a technical or functional skill set (that is enabled and reinforced systemically and culturally). Taking the earlier example of ADIA leadership development, the activities that collectively comprise the leadership work required to build the targeted capabilities are broader than selection and training, and include a careful selection of career experiences and developmental challenges that are supported by coaching, feedback, work redesign, and other supporting activities.

As ADIA or any other organization builds its capability plan, it must compare its current level of competence with the level of competence required to meet the desired capability. Is the current level of competence sufficient?

In some ways, we liken this step to the stress tests used by US and European banks to determine whether their financial capital is sufficient to deal with anticipated and unanticipated crises. Similarly, the competence-resourcing plan asks whether knowledge and human capital is sufficient.

Table 2-2 shows a simple framework for a competence-resourcing plan, utilizing the capabilities defined by ADIA. As the table indicates, ADIA leaders identified a number of specific technical and

TABLE 2-2

Assessing a capability resourcing plan: an example from ADIA

Capability	Vision	Key technical skill requirements	Potentially attractive areas for agile talent	Potential problems and risks
Prudent innovation	• Implement new and better investments that support our financial performance and national development goals	• Technical and organizational skills to effectively implement agreed upon initiatives and innovative investment and capability decisions	• Selection of long-term investment priorities • Partnership with innovation leaders in key growth areas • Strategic support in implementation	• Partner selection • Partner relationship effectiveness • Partner fit with ADIA culture and strategic goals
Effective collaboration	• Strong teamwork in and across ADIA units and with external resources	• Well-designed organization and strong skills at the leader and professional level in teamwork, collaboration, and information sharing	• Leadership training • Coaching • Work and organization design consulting support	• Alignment of priorities and activities with strategic goals and culture
Disciplined execution	• ADIA has the talent, leadership, and organization to meet and exceed its goals	• Leaders have the skills required to build, implement, and continuously improve organizational performance	• Strategy and operations support • Closing the vision-performance gap	• Ensure critical resources and organizational alignment needs, aligning resources in support

functional skills that are important in realizing the strategic organizational capabilities. The leaders also identified succession planning and performance assessment as areas of established internal expertise, while leadership training and coaching were limitations requiring improvement.

Molson Coors went through a similar process of capability and competence analysis. Although the company is a world-class company in terms of customer-centricity and product innovation, an internal assessment by its HR leaders identified the increasing importance of growth through acquisition and a gap in the skill set required for effective M&A. Although historically not crucial, consolidation has been a fundamental driver of market share and volume growth in the brewing industry. Unlike the four global majors—InBev, SAB Miller, Heineken, and Carlsberg—Molson Coors lacked the depth of M&A skills of its key competitors. Without these resources and skills, the company's growth through acquisition and its success at acquiring has been hampered. Consequently, Molson Coors is working hard to improve this capability.

Step 3: Clarify Areas of Expertise Where Agile Talent Offers Benefits

The third step in assessing your organization's capabilities focuses on which technical or functional skills are candidates for external resourcing, rather than full-time permanent employment. You can ask several questions in making this assessment:

- Why would we choose external resources over full-time employees?

- How specifically will external resources offer a superior benefit? Is the strategic measure time (e.g., we'll achieve the new product launch faster), cost (e.g., we'll reduce the cost of the new factory design), quality (e.g., we'll make a better product), or competitive challenge (e.g., we'll better avoid the competitive traps)?

- Is the skill requirement ongoing or time limited?

- How do we make sure that what we learn from the work of external partners is retained?

For ADIA, leadership training and coaching were identified as areas where external expertise was helpful, for a number of reasons. Partnerships with Harvard and INSEAD offered access to a wide range of world-class expertise otherwise unavailable to ADIA or only available at exorbitant expense. This external agile talent also brought up-to-date information on best practices within and outside the financial industry; for example, working with RBL Group enabled ADIA to tap into various global networks to build HR and leadership capability. And the use of agile talent made sense financially, given that leadership training and coaching could be offered on a part-time basis and would be structured to save cost without losing efficacy.

The fourth column of table 2-2 lists potentially beneficial areas for agile talent. Hence, ADIA's assessment of its capabilities flows from the identification of a capability, the vision for each capability, key technical skill "atoms" that make up the capability "molecule," and specific ways that agile talent may add to strategic performance readiness at ADIA.

Step 4: Identify Trade-Offs, Risks, and Other Potential Problems, and Plan Accordingly

The fourth key step in assessing a capability-resourcing plan is to identify what must be in place for agile talent resourcing strategies to achieve its goals. Consider a simple framework for assessing the likelihood of successful cloud resourcing. We have said that there are four factors that determine how well the organization turns its goals for agile talent into the reality of a well-oiled machine:

- Strategic alignment

- Performance alignment

- Relationship alignment

- Administrative alignment

Tool 2-2 helps leaders foresee any problems that might arise if problems of non-alignment are not resolved.

The ADIA case offers a useful perspective here. Collaboration was identified as a critical capability by ADIA leadership. The goal was greater teamwork among professionals across functions and asset classes and between internal staff and external experts brought in to work on a contract basis. To facilitate better collaboration, organization development consultants were originally brought in to address specific opportunities. When this first investment proved helpful, the organization hired

TOOL 2-2

Identifying potential problems of the four alignment categories

Alignment requirement	Potential problems	Impact if not addressed
Strategic		
Performance		
Relationship		
Administrative		

several senior consultants on a contract basis to work in ADIA. At first, ADIA leadership moved slowly and cautiously and focused on specific needs to win its managers' and other professionals' support for the use of this outside talent. Once the leaders earned that support, the benefits of a mixed solution comprising both external and internal competence has become evident to the broader ADIA team.

As with many things, this door leads to another door. Having clarified the capabilities needed to compete and win in the global marketplace, a company or agency now must design, or "curate," the solution. The organization's structure, relationships, leadership, culture, and work processes determine the practical, operational benefit that accrues from agile talent. For example, how congruent is the organization of work with the requirements of capability? Is performance management aligned? How well does the culture support and reinforce effective collaboration between internal staff and external experts? As Jim Sinegal, founding CEO of Costco, once said, "Culture is not the most important thing. It's the only thing," and Peter Drucker is famously reported to have said, "Culture eats strategy for lunch." Clearly, strategy, technical expertise in support of that strategy, and culture can't be traded off, but all are critically important. If organization structure, work systems, or well-implemented cultural values are absent, alignment suffers, and therefore the likelihood of real effectiveness is diminished.

The Architecture of Capability

Organizations can't be superior in all things, nor is it necessary to be so. We know from the work of both branding experts and human resources leaders that exceptional brands and leaders need to be distinguished in only a few areas of performance and can be middle of the pack in others. This logic of competing through capability also drives which capabilities provide meaningful superiority. This is the logic of competing through capability.

Although we talk about capability as if it is almost a uniform block, it ultimately has several components:

- **SHARED VALUES:** Do the parties involved in a capability understand and "feel" the vision and know why the capability is so critical? Does the team have a number of core stories that people tell one another and that shape the team's plans and dialogue?

- **STRATEGIC GOALS:** Does everyone know what needs to get done, and by when? And do people know the consequences of not being able to meet their obligation? Are the specific goals absolutely clear to all and reinforced through regular communication? Does everybody know his or her part and how the part makes or breaks the work of others and the whole? Does everyone have a clear line of sight to the vision—the "I did that"?

- **SKILLS:** Does the organization have the right number of people in the right locations with the right technical skills and the interpersonal skills needed to get the job done?

- **PERFORMANCE MANAGEMENT:** Are there good performance systems in place both to help leaders know that the work is progressing satisfactorily and to help them reliably attest that the team's actions will achieve the goal?

- **CULTURE:** Does the organization's culture support exceptional capability? Culture includes what leaders do and don't do, and how they do it. It means the work environment that an organization creates through the qualities (and quantities) of people it attracts, the standards it sets, how its leaders talk about obligations to the workplace and one another, which behaviors are rewarded and which are not, who is involved in which decisions, who sets priorities and policy, and who has and has shared (or withheld) what information from whom. Culture is the way that people interact with one another and the example set by the leaders.

- **COMMUNICATION AND INFORMATION:** How well and easily does critical information travel? Is communication easy and open or difficult and political? How well does management regularly provide information on the market and customers, and what external trends and events may affect the organization? How regularly does management seek the point of view of employees and external experts on what the business is doing, how the business is doing it, and what opportunities exist to improve?

- **WORK ORGANIZATION AND WORK SYSTEMS:** How is the work organized, and how are the individuals doing the work connected and aligned? Is the organization style of the business hierarchical, or does the structure reinforce empowerment and teamwork? How effectively designed are the work systems and processes of the organization?

- **PHYSICAL ASSETS:** Are the physical assets of the business in sync with the most important capabilities, or does the organization have to create significant work-arounds to get things done well and efficiently? Does the design and procurement of physical assets involve review and opinion by internal staff and external experts? What changes in physical assets would improve capability significantly?

For example, table 2-3 shows what IBM, recognized globally for developing its leaders, does to establish this capability. And Southwest Airlines reinforces customer centricity and cost efficiency as mutually related, key capabilities (table 2-4).

TABLE 2-3

IBM capability alignment: leadership

Capability	Approach
Shared values	IBM describes its strategic goal for leadership this way: "We invest in people and develop global leaders in a high-integrity environment."
Strategic goals	Every leader has a talent objective, which is one of the most intensely scrutinized objectives: Are you developing talented and engaged future leaders? Have you built a stronger team than you inherited?
Skill	IBM invests significantly in developing the skills of leaders in both good times and challenging times.
Performance management	IBM is known for rigorous performance management, but the process is tied to values as well as financial or operating achievement. The firm is well known for its focus on succession planning and leadership development; the IBM leadership model insists that leaders live the growth values.
Culture	IBM annually assesses all leaders against its growth values: external focus, clear thinking, imagination and courage, inclusiveness, and the development of expertise in oneself and others. By this means, the culture is reinforced by the systems of performance and development.
Communication and information	IBM takes great pains to communicate the importance of leadership, both externally and internally. Leadership is reinforced through the firm's significant investment in leadership and employee development. The CEO and other senior executives play an active role in leadership education and spend significant time in the classroom or supporting action-learning projects through IBM Executive School.
Work organization and systems	IBM reinforces its leadership capability in how it organizes and the freedom it gives general managers. Individuals are given the opportunity early on to run a business, and the organization is set up to give young leaders real responsibility in a true general management role early in their careers.
Physical or financial assets	IBM has made large financial investments in its service corps and executive corps.

Southwest Airlines' talent is different from the talent required by North American competitors like Delta, United, or American. These airlines all have the same focus on operations growth but have different customer value propositions. Delta, United, and American are competing for the same type of customer—business travelers who are willing to spend more to have nonstop flights and a potentially better seat

TABLE 2-4

Southwest Airlines capability alignment: cost and customer connectivity

Capability	Approach
Shared values	Southwest Airlines consistently beats the drum for its unique identity: low cost, low hassle, and good service by interesting and engaged employees.
Strategic goals	Southwest Airlines sees its goals of cost efficiency and customer connectivity as linked; on its website, the airline describes itself as "continuing to differentiate from other low-fare carriers through outstanding customer service."*
Skill	Southwest employees receive regular training, work in teams to identify opportunities for cost and service improvement, and operate in a multiskilled environment.
Performance management	Teams provide feedback to individual team members, and managers provide all employees with annual performance reviews and development discussions.
Culture	Southwest has a distinct culture. The airline is among the companies thats regularly score highest in employee surveys such as *Fortune*'s. The website reinforces the company's strong and enduring commitment to people and customers.
Communication and information	The organization rigorously measures and communicates to employees its performance in cost management, customer satisfaction, and employee engagement.
Work organization and systems	Work systems are designed to reinforce teamwork and collaboration in support of customer's experience, as well as cost efficiency. By working in teams, employees reduce turnaround time and cost by a substantial margin, which allows the airline to continue to charge low prices; in addition, attendants are invited to share their "talent," for example, singing and doing standup comedy, as a way of entertaining passengers.
Physical assets	Southwest decided to deploy fewer plane types than its competitors do in order to gain the cost benefit of reduced airplane downtime, labor force efficiency, employee multi-skilling, and reduced parts inventory costs. Southwest can turn its planes around quicker and keep them flying longer. Its fuel hedging strategy has saved the airline several billion dollars. Finally, employee engagement and work satisfaction has enabled the airline to operate its assets more cost-efficiently than would be the case in a more punitive union shop.

*Southwest Airlines, "Southwest Airlines at a Glance," *2011 Southwest Airlines One Report*, accessed July 18, 2015, www.southwestonereport.com/2011/?_escaped_fragment_=/thirty-thousand-foot-view/index#!/thirty-thousand-foot-view/index.

with dinner or lunch served. These three airlines are competing around service, not price. Emirates Airlines, in contrast, competes with a customer value proposition of quality. Anyone who has flown business class or first class on Emirates can attest to the luxury of spacious cubicles and the five-minute shower on long A380 flights for first-class passengers. Each of these definitions of how to win in the industry determines different capabilities and different kinds of talent.

Summary

In this chapter, we have described a disciplined and rigorous process for converting need and opportunity into decisions, plans, and specific actions that organizations must take to benefit from cloud resourcing of agile talent. As we've pointed out, external expertise is more available than ever before and can provide a unique expansion of expert resources. But the starting point is clarification of the organizational capabilities that are crucial to the organization's strategic goals. Capability, in turn, is far more than technical expertise—what we would call competency or specific skills. Capability addresses the combination of competence and culture and relies on the structure, work system, and other dimensions of organizational life to convert skill into the delivery of exceptional value.

Building capability is clearly not about optimizing the individual elements of the capability; the value lies in the integration of these elements. Integration makes the capability real in the eyes of both internal and external stakeholders, such as customers and employees.

Global competition, social forces, technology, demographics, and economics are driving faster and more dramatic change. These external factors manifest in different needs that are expressed by customers, investors, regulators, vendors, and communities. To meet these new needs and thus stay ahead, organizations must develop new capabilities. This environment of fast, dramatic change creates winners and losers. The winners are the companies that see the same trends that their competitors see but move faster to assemble the separate elements into capabilities. For example, IBM was in front with services a few years ago but missed the cloud opportunity. Nokia was the largest global cell-phone company and led in price but missed the early innovation window around smartphones and thus lost a huge opportunity.

The clearer a business can be about the capabilities it requires to win, the more creative it can be about the agile talent it needs to cultivate.

3

Refining the Strategy

Choosing the Right Approach to Agile Talent

The ADIA case in chapter 2 focuses on three issues of importance to any leader. First, does your organization have *world-class capability where it needs it most*, providing the muscle required for the organization to deliver on its strategic goals? Second, has the leadership team agreed on a *capability resourcing plan* that describes the technical and functional competencies required to close the organizational capability gap? And third, within the capability resourcing plan, *in what specific areas* can and should agile talent play a key role in meeting the needs for technical and functional expertise?

In this chapter, we provide the roadmap to refining the strategy, defining how specifically external expertise offers an attractive and meaningful alternative to full-time, fixed-cost staffing in key areas. In doing so, the chapter raises the fundamental resourcing question: What skills must we own and build, and where does it make sense to rent or lease?

Own, Rent, or Lease?

Some years ago, we were engaged to help the managing partner of a well-known global consulting firm review the firm's strategy and approach to staffing. As part of that work, we became interested in how organizations determined the right resource arrangements. Clearly, at that time, the bias was for full-time, permanent employees. But as outsourcing was just beginning to be taken seriously, we wondered how to bring a more strategic perspective to this approach. Specifically, we asked, under what circumstances might it be more effective and cost-efficient to "rent" expertise rather than "own" resources?

We noticed two fundamental factors at work. The first was the importance of the expertise to the organization—the extent to which a specific expertise is truly strategic to the mission and goals of the organization. Defining what is strategic is a very useful exercise. For example, Southwest Airlines, the first airline to recognize the impact of fuel price volatility, established a hedging program. By 2008, Southwest had saved over $3.5 billion in hedge benefits.[1] What made hedging strategic was the significant cost advantage it gave Southwest over other airlines. The resultant profits could be used to expand routes, acquire other airlines, and invest in new, more efficient, planes. In fact, for a few years, Southwest's market value was greater than the combined market value of all of its US airline competitors combined.

The second driver we recognized was uniqueness or availability: was the capability commonly available or rare? For example, Uber's ability to quickly move from selection to operation in new cities is a unique skill set that has given the ride-share company a significant first-mover advantage over Lyft or other mobile taxi-hailing services. Exxon Mobil's approach to high-tech reservoir modeling in oilfield exploration, and its

FIGURE 3-1

Strategic resourcing matrix: owning versus renting your talent

		Importance	
		Strategic	Nonstrategic
Availability	Unique or scarce	**1: Own** Own the best talent, and retain it	**2: Own** Deliver the basics at the lowest realistic cost
	Commonly available	**4: Rent** Rent the best talent, and set it up for success	**3: Rent** Contract out, and let procurement lead

ongoing investment in high-impact downstream refining technology, is unique to that company and allowed the company to increase production levels and efficiency beyond most competitors.

By contrast, California wineries will certainly agree that bottling is an important activity but a capability that is widely available. It must be done to specification, but beyond meeting standard at a competitive cost, there is not much advantage to owning bottling. So, bottling is typically a service provided to wineries by third parties.

When these factors of importance and availability are combined, a clear way to determine when to rent versus own emerges (figure 3-1). We call this the strategic resourcing matrix. Let's look at each quadrant of the guide in the figure.

Own the Best

Expertise that is both crucial to the performance and growth of the organization and unique and therefore difficult or impossible to accessible externally should, obviously, be owned by the organization.

Ownership makes sense for a number of reasons, mainly, the importance of the expertise and limited competitive access to the skill or
capability. But ownership isn't enough. If the capability is truly strategic, that is, if the performance and very existence of the company
depend on the expertise, the company must be more than merely very
good or excellent at this capability. Rolls-Royce airplane engines can't
just be good; they must be superior to what's available in the market
from competitors such as General Electric and United Technologies or
Rolls-Royce will not achieve its goals and may not survive. In short, if
the capability is both strategic and rare, the company needs to ensure
that the level of agile talent is consistent with the requirement—that
the talent is "best-in-world" to provide the competitive firepower that
is required.

Deliver the Basics

Delivering the basics is an invitation to focus on efficiency opportunities in work areas where the goal is "sufficiency" rather than excellence. All organizations have a variety of activities that must be done by
full-time staff. It may be the unique way the organization functions, a
legacy process that is easier kept than replaced, or the lack of available
alternatives in a market. However, the goal of any organization ought to
be to reduce the level of activity that is both nonstrategic and staffed
internally. This is especially the case where it is possible for the organization to cost efficiently make the organizational changes needed to
reduce full-time permanent staffing levels, or shift to a more appropriate mix of internal and external resources.

Statoil, the Norwegian international oil company, offers a useful
example here. As the cost of oil capture from the North Sea and other
locations has grown and as expertise has become far more available in
Norway, the HR department of Statoil increasingly turns to agile talent

when help is needed in a variety of specialist areas such as organization development—an important but not in the view of executives a truly strategic activity. Although there is some loss of insight and context, the organization benefits by engaging individuals who bring experience and innovation from other client organizations and thus benefit Statoil. In addition, tending to the needs of organization development this way allows Statoil to provide resources for this requirement on a variable-cost basis. This enables cost flexibility in responding to up and down economic cycles.

Contract Out

We would be remiss if we did not mention work that is nonstrategic, organized and performed in a standard way, broadly accessible, and therefore amenable to outsourcing. As others have observed, outsourcing makes the most sense when the work requires little performance monitoring and oversight other than contract compliance and is best managed by the purchasing function.

Rent the Best

The fourth category—rent the best—is a particular focus of this book. The increased availability of competence or expertise presents an interesting choice that is uniquely available to this generation of business leaders: should we buy or consider alternative resourcing methods, that is, should we own or rent? And if we decide to rent, where do we go to obtain the level of competence or expertise we need at an acceptable cost? In short, does it make good business sense to consider an agile talent solution?

This option has two steps, both of which are important: attracting the best external talent available, and setting them up for success. Both stages are important, and most organizations don't do a consistently good job of the latter stage. For example, both Hallmark and American Greetings are iconic publishers of e-cards and paper greeting cards. The two companies have established a strong design base and consider it critical to their success, but they also make extensive use of part-time or freelance design experts with titles such as "senior on-call creative retoucher." These individuals often receive training from the company to ensure that they provide the expertise needed, in the form required, to meet the unique needs of the company.

This category—rent the best talent and set it up for success—is where we find the greatest untapped opportunity for improving effectiveness and efficiency.

Apple: Reinforcing the Core

Apple's turnaround offers a useful example. When Steve Jobs returned to the company in 1997 after a twelve-year hiatus, it was evident that the organization had wandered from its innovative design roots. Among Jobs's first actions was rebuilding the Apple design team (it was sometimes known by insiders as the Apple Industrial Design Guild) and staff it with a core group of top design people. Next, he assembled a small group of key advisers and design consultants to advise on strategic design parameters (what they called "concept") and produce new product designs. Frog Design and IDEO are two of the better-known external partners Apple used, but the company brought in a variety of external resources that had a reputation for innovative work.

Jobs deeply understood the strategic importance of design; in fact, part of the "secret sauce" of Apple was how critical design was to Apple's brand—along with innovation—a critical strategic capability. Knowing he needed to "equip" the design team, he brought in world-class designers like Sir Jonathan Ive to lead and manage the function and to ensure that the external agile talent providing support to Apple under-stood the unique company philosophy and method of product design.

Apple recognized that expertise was commonly available in the marketplace and that an "Apple-ized" partnership of Apple design professionals with external resources would (1) offer arms and legs to get things done well and quickly, (2) provide an ongoing challenge to NIH ("not invented here") thinking—a factor that aligns nicely with our data about the value of agile talent as a tool for expanding the skill set—and (3) spur a friendly competition between internal and external experts. Extending the internal team with "rent the best" outside experts enabled Apple to focus its resources both strategi-cally and cost-efficiently. And by establishing retained relationships with these external firms, the company guaranteed the externals' continuing interest and engagement in the relationship and, there-fore, their best work.[2]

Banking on Agile Talent

Another useful example is National City Corporation, a large regional US bank now part of PNC Bank. One of us served as corporate SVP and chief learning and talent officer at National City. By 2005, National City's annual purchased services and expenses topped $1 billion; at that size, sourcing was identified as a strategic expertise lacking in the bank. A new head of procurement was hired from General Electric, and after doing some initial assessment, he suggested the goal of cutting purchased expenses by 10 percent without harming revenue functions or the customer experience. He built a small team of aggressive young finance analysts and extended the team's resources by expanding the network of agile talent through the cloud. And in so doing, he captured $100 million in savings.

Nike offers a third example of the choice to own or rent. The company engaged Damco, the A.P. Moller-Maersk logistics arm, to contract out the transportation of Nike goods to regional warehouses. But Damco identified an opportunity for Nike to better meet its sustainability goal by reducing its carbon footprint. The logistics company created the tools, trained the Nike staff, and monitored progress on behalf of Nike, providing Nike's supply chain team with helpful data to assess performance. By doing so, Damco moved from being just another logistics provider to a more influential role as a strategic partner.

These examples suggest some of the conditions that lead to a strategy of "own" or "rent the best." Table 3-1 lays out the conditions that would push a company toward owning or renting the talent that it needs.

The Nike example raises an additional point. These relationships are dynamic. The finding of strategy researchers from Rita Gunther McGrath to Gary Hamel is not just that change is accelerating but also that disruptive, paradigm-transforming change is accelerating. Damco transformed its relationship with Nike by creating unique competitive value; it did

TABLE 3-1

When to own the best talent, and when to rent it

Own the best, and develop and retain it	Rent the best, and set it up for success
• When the expertise is both strategic and required on an ongoing basis	• When outside expertise is available to the company
• When the expertise is unique to the company	• When the market offers the required level of expertise at acceptable cost
• When the need for the expertise is strong and its availability is rare and uncertain	• When the need for the expertise is term limited
• When the competency is crucial to the identity of the company or its offering and should not be shared with or made available to competitors	• When it is necessary to supplement a core team of internal experts
	• When internal experts have the skills to sponsor, guide, and manage the work of external experts
• When contracting with external experts is too costly, difficult, and uncertain	• When it makes sense to use external experts to train internal staff
• When the market cannot offer the level of expertise required or sufficient numbers	• When there is value in creating an internal-external partnership or in extending internal capability

what no other competitor was offering in a key corporate priority for Nike, and that has for at least a time made Damco a strategic partner.

Differing Goals

We have seen significant growth in full-out outsourcing—contracting out—over the past thirty years. But how well has it delivered on its promise? According to consultants KPMG, the data suggests that goals are generally underachieved. Table 3-2 presents the results of a recent study of five hundred executives.[3]

As the data suggests, contracting out—not surprisingly—focuses more on efficiency than other strategic capabilities. While 43 percent of the surveyed executives' organizations sought a reduction in operating

TABLE 3-2

How well conventional contracting out has delivered

Driver: how well has conventional contracting out delivered:	Percentage of executives surveyed whose organization uses contracting out for the purpose of meeting the listed mission-critical goal	Percentage of executives surveyed who believe that their organization was very effective in meeting the mission-critical goal through conventional contracting out
Reduced operating costs	43	31
Standardized processes	35	22
More effective operations at a global level	33	29
Transformed or reengineered processes	29	13
Increased access to talent	24	19
Increased access to new technology	22	20
Improved analytic capabilities	21	9
Forced change in business operations	17	14

Source: KPMG, "State of the Outsourcing Industry 2013: Executive Findings," company report, April 2013, http://www.kpmg-institutes.com/content/dam/kpmg/sharedservicesoutsourcinginstitute/pdf/2013/state-of-outsourcing-2013-exec-findings-hfs.pdf.

TABLE 3-3

The roles of agile talent in an organization's strategy

Role	Definition
Advisory	Expert guidance and advice provided to the organization on an occasional basis by a well-respected expert
Consultancy	Active, expert participation in a project or an initiative, with a defined scope, start, finish, and budget
Gig	Visiting experts; experts who are in residence in the organization for a specific project or event or for a defined period and who then leave
Retained relationship	A longer-term relationship to provide expert support over a longer time horizon and typically involving multiple projects
Cooperation agreement	A contractual agreement between two or more teams or organizations to share costs and benefits in addressing a common opportunity, problem, or initiative

costs and 35 percent emphasized standardization, only half these numbers viewed talent, technology, or analytics as a key goal.

What Solution Makes Most Sense When?

While contracting out is certainly as much a part of agile talent as any other category, it is less interesting to us in this book. The bigger opportunity in agile talent is the potential for bigger game—for strategic impact. But the larger question is what agile talent makes the most sense at which time? Table 3-3 lists and explains the various roles that agile talent can play in an organization's strategy.

Advisory

Advisers come in many forms, but all of them provide expert guidance and advice on an occasional basis, primarily but not always to the

senior management of an organization. A successful advisory relationship depends on the following characteristics:

- The topic is important enough for advice to be sought *and* followed.

- The adviser has the bona fides—the credibility and
  experience—to be seen as an expert with something important
  to say about the topic.

- The advice is seen as relevant and informative. Effective advice
  is a combination of three elements: a diagnosis, a statement of
  the implications for the organization, and an examination of
  alternative courses of action.

- The adviser must have a sponsor, a person of importance or
  influence in the organization and who is knowledgeable about
  the topic.

Beyond the traditional adviser, other types of advisory relationships
found today include the following:

- **MEMBERSHIP ON AN ADVISORY BOARD:** Through this
  relationship, a board member can provide insight to management
  in areas of importance. Advisory boards will be familiar to
  readers. Increasingly, organizations are forming advisory panels
  in key strategic areas and are becoming part of an organization's
  open-innovation approach. For example, one of us is a member
  of a global advisory panel for the Singapore Civil Service in the
  area of HR transformation. And because of recent mistakes, the
  US-based Centers for Disease Control appointed a panel of outside
  safety experts to correct sloppy procedures in US government
  labs. Finally, the use of external advisory panels by Procter &
  Gamble, 3M, and other companies in new research areas is
  frequently described as a key tool in open-innovation methods.

- **SPECIAL ADVISER:** General Atlantic, a private-equity firm, has advisory relationships with individuals who provide specific expert guidance in several technical areas, from M&A to digital marketing.

- **TECHNICAL ADVISER:** The photonics arm of NKT Group, a Danish holding company, has strong and deep relationships with a variety of technical advisers who help NKT Group define and evaluate new technologies. Similarly, Shell Oil reinforces its oil exploration and production performance through the help of an external technical review panel that engages with technical management and key technical staff.

- **THIRD-PARTY OVERSIGHT:** A recent breach in handling strains of anthrax and Avian Influenza led the Centers for Disease Control (CDC) in Atlanta to establish an independent advisory group body to review its practices on lab safety, recommend changes, and investigate worrisome breaches in the future

Consultancy

Great advisers create value by combining expert knowledge with organizational insight. Consultants share that challenge but have an additional burden. Unlike advisers, consultants work on projects with a beginning, an end, a schedule, deliverables, and a finite budget. Consultants need structure. Far more than advisers, consultants need the support of the organization to complete their task. Three considerations are particularly important:

- The purpose and deliverables of the work are well defined. The sponsoring executives define the deliverables of consulting in a clear and measurable way. In other words, when they are clear about the goals of the project or engagement, consultants can build an effective and efficient plan to objectively achieve the goals.

- There is clear sponsorship—ownership—of the work and the consulting relationship. The executive or executive team that has engaged the consultant has the formal power or informal influence to sponsor the initiative, and is able to provide the essential resources and political support needed to implement agreed recommendations.

- The expert resource or team understands how to get things done in the organization; otherwise, the goals are unlikely to be met.

So, advisers have ongoing, topically specific relationships with senior leaders and technical staff. Consultants, on the other hand, are project based: their expertise is applied against identified projects that have a beginning, an end, a typically tight schedule, well-defined deliverables, and a clear budget. Now we turn our attention to a third category of agile talent through cloud resourcing—the gigsters.

Gig

A talented young consultant we know left a promising career with his firm for an eighteen-month project requiring a move from Portland, Oregon, to Hong Kong. "The new company project is just too interesting to pass up," he said when asked at his exit interview. "It's not about the company; it's about a great project." Eighteen months later, he returned to the United States and to another employer offering—a project that was also "too interesting" to pass up.

The gig is a third category of agile talent and an area of significant growth for millennials and for Generation Z. We think of a gig as temporary employment, but it is really much more. As Tina Brown of the

Daily Beast described it, the gig economy reflects the *assembly of a career* based on interesting projects. In other words, gigsters—like our talented young consultant who traveled to Hong Kong—are all about "cool work." We first heard this description in a talk given by Libby Sartain, a well-known HR executive. She talked about the decreasing number of young professionals she meets who are interested in a permanent, full-time role in an organization.

Julia (name changed) is a good example. She graduated from University of California, Berkeley, and received her law degree from Yale University with a focus on international law and arbitration. After an unsatisfying tour of duty in a top US law firm, she gave up the office and big paycheck to seek a more interesting opportunity. She is a career assembler, as Brown put it, and holds multiple part-time jobs: she is working as a part-time gigster on a significant legal case for a small boutique law firm; she is developing the plan for an exciting nongovernmental organization and is actively raising funds. And she is an unpaid coach on international arbitration to third-year students of a leading law school.

Gigging is often found in unexpected places. For example, according to recent data, only 35 percent of adjunct faculty in US universities are interested in a full-time role at the university.[4] The majority prefer the flexibility of remaining adjunct. New forms of gigging have appeared over the last few years. A recent favorite of ours is in Scotland, where the national government recently inaugurated a program it calls "geek in residence."[5] The program places developers and designers with forward-looking cultural organizations for a defined period, and for a specific project. Author Andy Young describes an example: "For her residency with the National Theatre of Scotland (NTS), Kate Ho brought with her a toolbox full of tech. She ran a session with staff, introducing the group to augmented reality and work using Microsoft Kinect. . . It's a simple idea, but the impact was incredible. Having seen

what augmented reality was capable of, the NTS team could imagine
how it might be integrated with more traditional media such as theatre
scripts."[6]

Why would organizations seek a gigster rather than a consultant or
full-time employee? One purpose is talent attraction: a gig is a way many
organizations have attracted top talent, offering them interesting work
that sometimes leads to a full-time employment offer. It is also a way
to attract highly talented individuals who don't want full-time employment but who are attracted by interesting or challenging project work.

Retained Relationship

A retained relationship is a relationship between organizations that
may include advisory, consulting, and even gigster-like support and
that provides a broader range of services or guidance. An early example
is the relationship that Bain & Company created with a variety of cor-
porations, eventually leading some, like Dell, to release their planning
function to ongoing Bain support.

There are a variety of forms of retained relationship, including the
following:

- **PREFERRED PARTNER:** Various institutional relationships
  between organizations might be described as preferred partner.
  One obvious example is the audit relationship between an
  industrial organization and its accounting firm. Another is a close
  relationship between a management team and a consulting firm.
  An organization like TASC—a Northrup Grumman spin-off and
  now named Engility—or Booz Allen Hamilton essentially supplies
  technical experts to US government departments, from the
  Department of Health and Human Services to the Department
  of Defense. Slalom, a quickly growing Seattle-based consultancy,

offers what it describes as "staff augmentation." These firms and others like them essentially provide agile talent on a mass scale.

- **DEDICATED TEAM:** Just as brokerages are increasingly making available new investment options for their clients through open architecture, they are also bringing on intact teams to provide ongoing investment services on a contracted basis. For example, a team might manage a mutual fund or an investment portfolio on behalf of the brokerage's customers. In his book *Chasing Stars*, Boris Groysberg talks at length about the determinants of success and failure in these relationships.[7]

- **SUBSCRIPTION-BASED TECHNICAL INSIGHT:** A variety of firms provide ongoing technical insight to organizations and investors on a subscription basis. Gartner, for example, provides updates and predictions to thirteen thousand client organizations in eighty-five countries through its fifteen hundred analysts.

As retained relationships increase, getting the value from this version of agile talent requires the leadership attention of both service providers and corporate clients. Smart external-resource providers— whether they are individuals, teams, or larger organizations—will ask themselves: "Are we set up to offer the quality of relationship we need to provide our client organizations?" And, they will do so through rigorous processes of regular review, enabling them to identify and close any important experience and performance gap.

But, it's not enough for the providers to take care of their end of the relationship. Corporate and public-sector organizations must rigorously select the right external talent, establish effective roles and relationships that facilitate success, and ensure the sponsorship, feedback, and engagement needed to keep the work on the right track, with the right momentum.

A second challenge is specific to retained relationships, but also affects advisers and consultants. As Robert Mautz and Hussein Sharaf noted in their book *The Philosophy of Auditing*, "the greatest threat to [the auditor's] independence is a slow, gradual, almost casual erosion of [this] honest disinterestedness."[8] This cautionary statement is just as relevant to individual experts, teams, and firms outside the audit business. A retained relationship is only as effective as the ability of the expert or firm to grow with the client and see its strategic strengths, challenges, and culture—in the here and now.

Cooperation Agreement

Cooperation agreements are another way to obtain agile talent. Why would an organization choose a cooperative resourcing solution? The advantage of a cooperative agreement is the ability to learn from the research of many relevant organizations; the disadvantage is the obligation that each organization must put its learning into the communal pot, so to speak, and the ongoing investment of time, cost, and sharing of knowledge. But when the agreement is well thought-out, the value of cooperation can be significant. For example, the RBL Group has created the RBL Institute, which is a cooperation of fifty leading global companies mutually focused on sharing knowledge and innovation in the human capital and leadership space.

Three Approaches to Agile Talent

Ten years ago, IBM was at the top of its game in technology and services. Now it is seen as a laggard in cloud and mobility computing and investing billions of dollars to catch up. For IBM, agile talent provides a means of quickly establishing capability in new and fundamentally

TABLE 3-4

Types of agile-talent arrangements, and the purposes underlying each

Establish expertise; get started	Leverage expertise; build strategic capability	Transform capability; create a powerful reputation
• A key area of required expertise is lacking.	• The organization has solid strength in the areas required for strategic organization capability.	• The expertise is crucial to the strategic performance of the organization.
• The expertise is a skill area that is important to establishing strategic organizational capability.	• The capability is clearly or increasingly strategic.	• The organization has real expertise combining internal and external experts, but needs to significantly increase impact.
• The need for this expertise is likely to increase over time. The organization must establish capability in this area and must own a core competence and supplement, as required, by renting.	• The organization recognizes the performance value of the capability to strategic growth and performance.	• The leadership undertakes an assessment of how to take capability to the next level.
• As the strategic need becomes more evident, the organization must define the balance of external and internal expertise resourcing.	• Leadership defines the future requirement of this capability.	• The organization establishes a clear vision for capability growth, and identifies the "as is–to be" gap that must be closed.
	• The organization determines the best mix of internal and external expertise.	• The organization implements a change management strategy to close the gap, build unique capability, and communicate both internally and externally.
	• The organization takes action to obtain, monitor, and sustain the expertise needed.	

strategic markets. KKR, the private equity giant, has a strong track record in compliance, but the US government has increased its reporting demands. KKR is reaching out to a number of legal and accounting firms to supplement its capability in compliance. Uber is going full out to grow and protect its capability of immediate availability of service through a network of thousands of freelance drivers.

Each of these examples reflects a particular strategic use of agile talent. As table 3-4 points out, the first—reflected in the IBM example—is utilizing agile talent to get started or get in the game. The second, which we call leveraging expertise, is a thoughtful and strategic mix of both internal and external talent, working together toward a common goal. KKR and other financial services firms have taken this approach in areas like compliance. Finally, as a third approach, some organizations have chosen to be all in, seeing the opportunity to utilize agile talent in partnership with internal expertise to establish a powerful reputation for the capability and remain on the cutting edge. Uber is a prime example of this trend, and as an innovator is at the front line of dealing with the obstacles to change.

Summary

The purpose of this chapter was to describe architecture of agile talent and the arrangements that organizations select to meet their short- and longer-term strategic goals. In combination with the earlier chapters, we have set the table for a more granular discussion of the impact of agile talent on how organizations resource, organize the work, and engage work colleagues—internal or external—in common cause. Now that we have examined why agile talent is an attractive resourcing solution, and the variations on how it is best applied, the remaining chapters focus on how to align organizations to achieve the outcomes that attracted them to agile talent. As our pilot study data indicated, there are significant opportunities for organizations and their leaders to better plan, welcome, orient, and reinforce the work of external resources and, therefore, to take significantly greater advantage of the power of agile talent. In the next three chapters, we describe how companies can better select, attract, and retain external agile talent. We also look at how the organization's talent management philosophy and methods affect the quality of collaboration between internal and external resources. We describe how top organizations meaningfully engage external resources rather than treat them in a more transactional (and often suspicious) manner. The chapters also examine how the structure and work methods of the organization facilitate or impede the performance of external experts. Finally, we recommend what leaders must do exceedingly well to get the most from their investment in agile talent.

4

Attracting and Welcoming Agile Talent

Orienting External Talent to Your Organization

Chances are that your organization has recently talked with an external expert, perhaps someone with strong cyber security skills to assess whether your systems are fully secure. Your organization needs the help—stories about the impact of stolen customer information have damaged the reputation of companies like Target, The Home Depot, and Citibank. This expert is arguably one of the best, is in high demand, and her daily contract fee is higher than you expected. But she has a reputation for being exceedingly smart, working fast, and coming up with innovative solutions. You are ready to contract with her.

What plans have you made to ensure that the high cost of this external agile talent is returned many times over in contribution? What environment have you fashioned to ensure that your organization gets the greatest possible value from the work? Can your organization, in turn, provide an experience that leads the expert to feel good about your company and the work? Will she be inclined to sing the praises of your organization to other organizations?

More Than the Money

The chances are good that in India (where over 50 percent of the people are under twenty-five, and 65 percent under thirty-five) or many other parts of Asia, your external resource will be a millennial or perhaps even from Generation Z. If a millennial, the person is likely to be focused primarily on the opportunity and its potential to be interesting work that makes a difference. Money is important, but the scarce resource for millennial experts is the work and work environment. These individuals have high expectations for their supervisors and colleagues and want a challenge that is worthwhile. They expect a lot from the work they do, how they are managed, and the organization for which they are working. And they are unafraid to leave an organization that does not keep its promises.

Recently, a young tech expert named Jordan Price explained to *Huffington Post* readers why he had quit his contract position at Apple that very day:

> This morning I got up a bit later than usual, and I missed the one Apple bus that stops by my house. I was thankful I didn't have to drive every day. But I was still thinking that I'd rather be taking my daughter to her preschool like I did on some mornings before I started at Apple. I got into work and immediately had to go to another meeting. It went fine, and then I got back to my desk. Without so much as a hello, my boss hit me with another weird

low-blow insult wrapped up nicely as a joke. I tried to ignore it and get back to work, and I realized I just couldn't focus at all on my job. I was too caught up thinking about how I should deal with the situation. Should I put in my notice? Could I make it to the end of my contract? Could I switch to a different team? How could I find a new job if I was always stuck in Cupertino? Maybe I should bop my punk boss in his nose? No don't do that, Jordan.

Then at lunch-time I wiped the iPad data clean, put the files I had been working on neatly on the server, left all their belongings on my desk, and I got in my car and drove home. I left a message for my boss and told him he's the worst boss I had ever encountered in my entire professional career and that I could no longer work under him no matter how good Apple might look on my résumé. The third-party company that contracted me is furious because I've jeopardized their relationship with Apple, and of course they feel that I've acted highly unprofessionally by walking out. I'm not really proud of myself for doing that, and I do feel terrible for destroying the long relationship I had with the recruiter who helped me land the interview. This is all an especially difficult pill to swallow because I was so excited to work for Apple. I'm not sure if this will haunt me or not, but all I know is that I wanted to work at Apple really bad—and now not so much.[1]

Russ Mitchell, writing in *Fast Company*, offered the following description of motivation for many technical experts:

As important as money is to tech people, it's not the most important thing. Fundamentally, geeks are interested in having an impact. They believe in their ideas, and they like to win. They care about getting credit for their accomplishments. In that sense, they're no different from a scientist who wants credit for work that leads to a Nobel Prize. They may not be operating at that exalted level, but the same principle applies.[2]

Price and Mitchell make it clear that today's experts have different expectations of work and career. Whether the talent is working for a consultancy like Bain, is an independent creative for hire to advertising firms, or is a cyber-security guru, both recently minted and more experienced experts may now be less interested in a career with a particular organization and far more focused on the present employee experience. This attitude shouldn't be surprising, given the cynicism of those who were either caught during the Great Recession of 2008 or who watched as friends and family lost jobs and then their faith in the companies that had employed them. For top candidates and performers, cynicism has given way to expectations that are more explicit. What must organizations do to increase their attraction to outstanding external talent?

What Is Your Offer?

A couple of years ago, one of us led a strategic review of a midsize European industrial conglomerate. The board sought a path to make the firm a more attractive acquirer of companies. But the firm had an unclear value proposition made worse by doing a poor job of communicating what made the conglomerate an attractive resource for growing companies. To make matters worse, the firm was far clearer about what it expected from acquisitions than it was about what made it a better "home" or owner than other investors. In short, it needed a compelling answer to the real question that its value proposition should have emphatically answered: "Why should any company want to be acquired by us?"

The same basic question should be asked by executives who are selecting and attracting top expert talent: Why would a top adviser, a consultant, or other agile talent want to work for our company? What have we done to establish a relationship and provide an experience that would motivate a talented external partner to give us his or her best work and full engagement?

In an increasingly competitive world, top talent goes where there is the greatest potential for both satisfaction and career opportunity. Answering the preceding questions meaningfully, and communicating the answers regularly and consistently, requires an *employee value proposition*. Think of the proposition as the "give and get" for membership in the organization, essentially a contract between the individual and the organization. For example, Airbnb, sporting a $10 billion valuation as of 2014 (and more since), understands the importance of articulating—in terms that are meaningful to young software engineers—what working at its growing company offers:

> Airbnb is the world's largest marketplace for space, and we keep getting bigger every day. With 10 million nights booked and counting, we're constantly tackling challenges in search algorithms, payments, fraud prevention, and growth—all while maintaining a beautiful user experience. We want to build solutions to these problems that are scalable, performant, and elegant, and we're looking for talented people to help us do just that.
>
> Every engineer deploys on his or her first day—and every day after that too. We use Amazon Web Services and practice continuous deployment so we can quickly try out new ideas and iterate on existing product features, and we love experimenting with new technology if it's right for the job. Not only do we ride the cutting edge, we make it: we've open sourced Rendr, a JavaScript

framework that lets Backbone.js apps render seamlessly on both the client and the server, and Chronos, a distributed fault-tolerant scheduler that runs on top of Apache Mesos, among other projects. Our engineers regularly present at conferences around the country.

Learn together. We believe that engineering is a continuous process of learning and improvement, and that the best way to learn is by getting help from your fellow engineers. All of our engineers hang out in Campfire so that we can keep informal knowledge sharing (and meme bombing) flowing—and because coding is more fun when you do it together. We host biweekly tech talks, both internal and external, so that everyone gets a chance to become the best at their craft.

Pixelwax. That's our word for the dedication and craftsmanship we bring to our work. For us, engineering isn't just a job but a practice that we want to perfect. We aim to keep our systems modular, our code clean, and our documentation clear, and we follow the Cub Scout philosophy of leaving things better than you found it. It's not just about the code—putting the right processes and tools in place to make developers happy and efficient is important to us because it gives us the time to focus on polishing the product.[3]

Airbnb gets it. The company understands that a good employee value proposition is not an advertising pitch; it is a description of what the organization commits to provide individuals who do work for the organization. In making this commitment, Airbnb is paying close attention to the expectations of millennials, but Airbnb's employer brand isn't just the marketing blah-blah we typically find in brand statements. The management understands that it is, in fact, a promise: "Here is what you can expect of us if you work here and you perform well."

As importantly, Airbnb isn't only talking to candidates for full-time employment. It understands Silicon Valley as an ecosystem of techies who are in, out of, and between organizations, and its message is meant to reach external agile talent as well as potential traditional employees.

More of the world is headed in the direction of Airbnb, focusing less on the traditional employment arrangement and more on talent however it is best found and arranged. In a world of agile talent, the term *employee value proposition* is insufficient because it focuses on the traditional relationship between full-time employee and employer. We prefer the term *employer brand.* In an environment where external expertise accounts for an increasing percentage of FTEs, it makes sense to encompass both traditional employees and agile talent. As with other dimensions of branding, a targeted communications outreach is important to attract and retain the talent you need.

Describing the brand is the first step. Setting the organization up to live the brand is the bigger challenge. As Tom Davenport of Babson College points out, a powerful brand statement differentiates the organization from competitors only if the promise is real.[4] HR consulting firm Towers Watson concurs that brand realization is easier said than accomplished; in fact, less than half the organizations it polled have an explicit plan to live their employer brand.[5]

When we talk with executives, we find the same broad categories that were observed by Ed Schein and Lotte Bailyn of MIT in their 1970s research on career anchors and expanded by Brook Derr at Brigham Young University as career orientations. We uncovered an additional career orientation in our interviews: a growing number of young and well-established professionals are committed to meaningful service and want to make a social contribution in their work. Thus, today's organizations can offer their agile talent six employer brand categories, or what we call *majors* (figure 4-1).

FIGURE 4-1

Employer branding majors

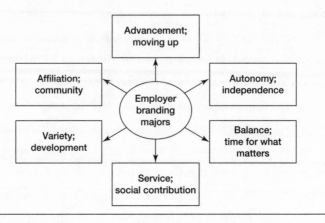

What emphases do these six majors reflect?

- **ADVANCEMENT**: a motivation to advance in role, status, and
  financial achievement. Individuals attracted by this employer
  brand are looking for organizations that will provide significant
  and ongoing advancement opportunity, either by rising in an
  organization or "punching their career ticket." In other words, "I
  want to join your organization because it offers me the opportunity
  to progress to greater responsibility, influence, and position."

- **AFFILIATION**: a commitment to an organization. Whereas
  advancement-oriented individuals are willing to trade off loyalty
  for reward or opportunity, affiliation-oriented individuals trade
  off reward for a sense of belonging and team. In other words,
  "I want to join your organization because it offers me security
  (based on my contribution) and a feeling of community and
  belonging."

- **AUTONOMY**: a drive for independence. Autonomy-driven
  individuals seek an organization that offers greater self-direction

in what they work on (think 3M or Google's providing 15 percent self-directed time), how they work on it, and where and when they work. In other words, "I want to join your organization because I have the freedom to do my job on my own schedule, and in my own way."

- **VARIETY**: an interest in variety and challenge in one's work and a desire for support for professional development. Individuals want newness and fear the boredom of repetitive work. They are eager, career-long learners. In other words, "I want to join your organization because I will have the chance to learn and do different things and be consistently challenged by new problems and interesting projects."

- **BALANCE**: the desire to balance work, family, and other priorities. Perhaps an individual has a new child, an elderly parent in need, or a life interest that is important. Individuals seeking balance are not less committed to performance, but want a life beyond work. In other words, "I want to join your organization because, as important as work is, it is not all of my life and I will have the opportunity to balance job contribution with my other life interests."

- **SERVICE**: a motivation to contribute to society or a community directly or indirectly through work. We added this brand major to the original five categories. Individuals with this focus want to create a life that combines work and service and are most interested in offering their expertise to organizations that are invested in a broader social agenda. In other words, "I want to join your organization because my work enables me to make a positive contribution to society and to give back in a way that is meaningful to me."

Derr's research found four important trends with respect to career orientations. First, individuals are almost always a mix of orientations, and for good reason. Success in life, as the psychiatrist Karen Horney reminded us, requires flexibility in how we respond to situations. Second, most but not all individuals have a distinct brand major as well as one or more brand "minors." Third, there is no credible evidence of a strong correlation between performance and an individual's orientation. Fourth, orientation mix and majors can and often does change over an individual's lifetime. It's not uncommon, for example, for a person's strong advancement orientation to morph into a greater need for balance as growing children or aging parents make demands.

These trends are easily applied to the employer brand concept. As with individual orientations, the offer is never one thing. There is a major; for example, the high expectations and competitive environment of a company like McKinsey or Goldman Sachs speak loudest to people attracted by advancement. Organizations have different ways of reaching the summit of their industry; there is no one path. And employer brand majors can change over time as industry dynamics and competitive requirements change.

Particularly in older, more established organizations, we often find ambiguity or conflict in employer brands. Ambiguity reflects the lack of a clear major; when all brands are minor, there is no clear brand. If this is the case, the leadership team must give thought to the relationship between employer brand and the career orientations that are signaled in the brand statement. For example, organizations such as Exxon Mobil traditionally appeal to the "secure" career orientation and primarily seek career-minded technologists who want to make a commitment to a career in a particular company. Twitter, by contrast, generally focuses more on advancement and variety. The US Department of State is particularly attracted to high-caliber individuals who are looking for a career in service and prepared to live in many different environments in order to do so.

However, all orientations need to be respected and cultivated, or problems inevitably arise. For example, one global firm used Derr's career orientations in a leadership program with its high-potential engineering talent. These engineers had been hand-selected as the most likely future leaders of the company. Most of them had primary career orientations around variety, autonomy, service, and balance. Several of the senior leaders of the company attended the end-of-day wrap-up and heard an overview of the orientations. Most of these senior leaders were oriented toward advancement and affiliation. Without knowing the orientation scores of the high-potential engineers, one of the senior executives summarized his own feelings: "I hope a few of you want advancement, but if not, I like the variety orientation because you are likely the best technically and might discover something commercial for us. The affiliation orientation is good too because you are loyal and the backbone of our company. But I hope we don't have many of you with the other orientations—those driven by autonomy are likely to be difficult to work with, and those emphasizing balance don't sound very committed to hard work."

Unintentionally, this senior executive signaled to the future leaders of the company to disguise their orientations if theirs were different from his. In a world of choices for the best talent, this narrow approach is a huge mistake. Agile talent will find places where it can be all it wants to be without fear of retribution or unconscious bias.

Employer Branding: Closing the Gap

We've found that a five-step process best serves leaders in defining and implementing a powerful employer brand to create an employee value proposition (figure 4-2).

FIGURE 4-2

Building an employer brand

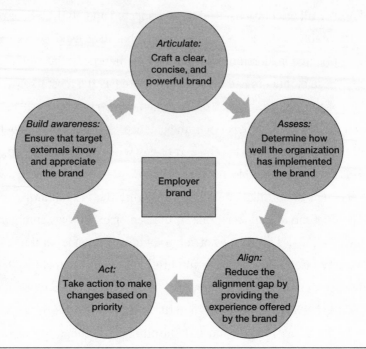

Step 1: Articulate

What is your organization's brand major? To create an accurate, powerful answer to this question, take one hundred points, and distribute them among the six orientations described earlier. Then, looking at this distribution, craft a clear and succinct brand statement that incorporates the promise your organization is making to external experts as well as employees and that describes both the major and the minor brand. In a LinkedIn blog post, Lydia Abbot compiled some good examples of edgy, funny YouTube videos that companies have created, portraying themselves as a desirable place to work.[6]

Step 2: Assess

The second step is to assess in general terms how well the systems and practices of your organization currently support the direction of the brand. Three basic questions are particularly helpful:

- In what specific ways are we clearly living our brand?

- How are we demonstrably not living the brand, and how do we need to change?

- Finally, in what ways do we send a mixed message and need to resolve the confusion?

Many organizations find it helpful to involve feedback from both internal staff and external experts. However the feedback is obtained, it's important to be as objective as possible. Tool 4-1 outlines a typical agenda for a focus group to discuss these three important questions about an organization's brand.

TOOL 4-1

Getting feedback on your employer brand

A typical focus group agenda: 90 minutes

The meeting is led by a facilitator, who is also the recorder. The group typically includes six to nine individuals, who may be internal employees, as well as part-time and gig employees:

Step 1 (30 minutes): Overview of the employer brand statement drafted by leadership, including Q&A

Step 2 (about 45 minutes): Facilitator begins a group discussion:

- What is the message we think the brand sends to internal staff? What is the brand statement we're sending to external colleagues who may be working with us?
- What changes in the brand statement do we suggest? Why?
- What changes in how we operate are appropriate given the intention of the brand statement?

Step 3 (about 15 minutes): Facilitator reviews the discussion, identifies key areas of agreement, and describes next steps, e.g., review with management

Step 3: Align

In this step, you address specific needs for change or improvement—needs identified in the prior step. It's most useful to focus on priorities that both reinforce the brand and create real benefit. As in the previous step, simple questions work best:

- What do we need to start doing to more fully live the brand?

- What do we need to stop doing to more fully live the brand?

- What do we need to do differently?

- Finally, what is working well and should be continued?

Step 4: Act

In this step, you need to address the priority areas for improvement in actualizing or reinforcing the brand. For example, one large consulting firm had identified entrepreneurship as a critical focus for improvement and signaled its importance by reinforcing entrepreneurship as a key indicator of high potential. But, as a result, many senior managers in contention for partnership tightly controlled client relationships to demonstrate their readiness for promotion to partner. Hence, the organization had to find a way to give more junior staff the opportunity to sell and learn how to sell services.

Step 5: Build Awareness

Creating the brand is certainly the first step, and the organization must give it life and integrity. But an active effort to publicize the brand is essential. You need to build and execute a communications plan that answers the question "How will we spread the news about the good work we are doing in living our brand?"

Leaders Must Show the Way

An organization's increasing use of external talent becomes obvious to full-time employees. They may be anxious, annoyed by a revolving door of consultants, or happy to work with external experts, but they always have some reaction to external talent, and the reaction needs to be addressed through communication by management.

The first step in making change is recognizing the need for change. Leaders play a critical role here by clearly communicating how the total workforce is evolving and why. What does this communication look like? Some of the information employees need are the strategic facts, the skills the organization needs to deliver on the business strategy and key priorities, the availability of these skills, and the numbers. Leaders must articulate a plan and logic for the organization's resourcing philosophy: what it is, is not, and what the strategy and philosophy means in practical terms. For example, if competitive requirements are rapidly changing, how will that affect the mix of full-time and contingent work? And what does this mean for people in different parts of the organization?

Assess the Culture

For organizations that expect or need to depend more on agile talent, leadership communication—articulating the direction and its importance—is not the same as making it so. Leaders who seek the greatest possible performance from their investment in external experts must take a hard look at the culture and the experience of outsiders joining their organization. Fundamentally, it means revisiting how external experts are treated from the minute of agreement on a working relationship to the last wave good-bye and onto the new opportunity. Is the culture of the organization—in general and specifically for cloud resourcing—one that really compels the fullest possible skill, creativity, and best effort of external experts?

For an organization that has historically emphasized full-time employees, the cultural shift may be a challenging one. Organizations vary in their philosophy of resourcing. Exxon Mobil is a historically diehard *developer company*, one that had the financial resources to hire whatever expertise was deemed necessary.

Exxon still primarily relies on a grow-your-own philosophy of resourcing. Organizations like it have a cultural dilemma that they must address as more external experts are engaged. The dilemma is one of trust: there are two types of people, "us" and "not us." Trust is difficult for these organizations when they are dealing with external experts (after all, the externals are "not us") and deploy them as a pair of hands to be managed actively and monitored carefully. As a consequence, the organizations are less open to the advice and experiences of external experts and more likely to manage agile talent for compliance with the statement of work than for commitment and engagement.

To change the culture, leaders must show the way. How managers talk about external resourcing, respond to and participate in decisions about external resources, and interact with externals sends a powerful message. Employees have a sharp ear and hear what managers are saying or implying between the lines. For example, a senior leader at a *Fortune* 100 company thought it was clever to refer to consultants as "insultants" and did so regularly, often in meetings that his consultants attended. The rancor of his statement was not lost on his direct reports, who followed his lead and were equally antagonistic. Not surprisingly, the project was difficult and ultimately a failure. Managers need to watch the signals they send. They must effectively communicate why they are bringing in external experts, the specific value added that externals will provide and that internal staff cannot, and the importance of good collaboration.

There are many examples of good modeling by leaders. One we found particularly impressive followed from work our consulting firm did for a large international petrochemical company. Briefly, the goal was to reduce the annual run rate cost by $100 million dollars. The company was very successful with this project—it captured more than the amount required and did so without significant layoffs. We were surprised and delighted when the leadership of the company, and the forty-five internal managers and specialists involved in the project, hosted a celebration of the consulting team. The cost of the celebration was a mere rounding error in comparison with the savings obtained by the project. But the social event reinforced relationships that continue to this day and sent a powerful message to the organization: external experts can be partners too.

Orienting Your Agile Talent: Setting Them Up for Success

Important organizational processes have well-defined and well-documented scripts. There is no doubt about the steps required for finance to close the month or for complaints about managerial abuse to be investigated. Organizations are generally utilizing external agile talent more frequently, but it is new enough that there is little discipline around the process during and after contracting.

An effective orientation is essential to both early performance and the acceptance of the external resource. And as described in chapter 3, a thorough orientation to the company is not consistently provided when companies take on external talent. Kevin Murphy, CEO of Driscoll's, the largest berry company in the world, is a good example of how to bring external talent onboard the right way. As part of the preparation for a leadership development offsite with our team at RBL Group, Murphy met with us to talk about his company's vision, mission, and values before we talked about his goals for leadership development. There is nothing unique about Driscoll's vision, mission, and values other than the company's belief in them and its dedication to make decisions according to those principles. After meeting with Murphy for two hours, we found ourselves converted to what Driscoll's wants to do. Here's what he talked about:

DRISCOLL'S

Our Vision

To become the world's berry company, enriching the lives of everyone we touch.

Our Mission

To continually delight Berry Consumers through the alignment with our Customers and our Berry Growers.

Our Values

The nature of our very competitive business demands a lot from the people committed to it. There are three traits we prize most highly in our collective effort to create a special future:

Passion: The passion to excel and accomplish great things.
Humility: The humility to respect and learn from our colleagues and competitors.
Trustworthiness: The trustworthiness that transforms our dependence upon one another into our greatest strength.

Getting the consulting team onboard at Driscoll's was incredibly simple. The CEO and his key staff invested the time to tell us why our work was important and how it contributed to the strategic and operational challenges facing the company. The CEO's comments linked our work to the vision and mission of the company and how specifically the work would add to its competitiveness. This clear communication was a strong signal of employer branding. Not surprisingly, the result of the onboarding—and the ongoing communication and engagement that followed—meant that the team cared far more about the work. As one team member commented, "We've been given the challenge of making a significant contribution to a business that takes us and our work very seriously. Let's deliver 'amazing.'"

Our data says that organizations benefit when they do an effective job of preparing external resources like the consulting team at Driscoll's. Our pilot study indicates an almost perfectly normal distribution; approximately an equal number of executives feel good or less than good about the quality of orientation and onboarding provided to external resources. This frequent lack of adequate orientation is problematic. The likelihood of project success is significantly diminished when external resources operate without a clear understanding of the organizational and cultural challenges of project success.

In figure 4-3, the respondents fall into three approximately equal groups; about a third of executives describe their organization as effective, a third see their organization as acceptable on this factor, and a third indicate concern. What is the cost of inadequately preparing advisers, consultants, or other agile talent to perform? We may reasonably assume that it is far more than the time and dollar cost of doing a proper job.

This is a critical point. If organizations do not do a good job of orienting external experts in the organization's culture, values, and way of doing work, the likelihood of the agile talent's success is substantially reduced. A variety of sources have found that 70 percent of change

FIGURE 4-3

Effective orientation for onboarding external talent

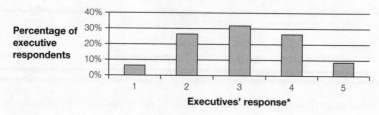

Source: Pilot study by RBL Group.

*Responses from the RBL pilot survey of 200 executives answering the question "Do you orient your external resources sufficiently to the organization and culture?" on a scale of 1 to 5, where 1 = not very effectively, 3 = neutral, and 5 = very effectively.

initiatives typically fail to achieve their goals, although the plans and methods of a substantially higher 90 percent of projects are technically sound. Culture and relationships are the outlier challenge, and the ability of external resources to understand, appreciate, and accommodate the unique nuances of an organization's culture and build effective relationships with internal staff is typically the make-or-break dimension of success in agile talent resourcing.

A recent guidebook by the Society for Human Resource Management and other publications describe what a good orientation accomplishes.[7] Building on their description, after effective orientation, external talent should be able to respond affirmatively to the points below:

- I UNDERSTAND WHAT IT MEANS TO BE A RESPECTFUL GUEST. This relates to company policies, legal regulations, and the relevant culture. For example, working in another country or in a religiously affiliated organization may challenge the knowledge of external resources, where ignorance of customs would be problematic.

- I UNDERSTAND THE PROJECT AND WHY IT IS IMPORTANT. As we've discussed, external experts today are concerned about both the meaningfulness of their work and the implementation and impact of their efforts. Helping externals understand why the organization is sponsoring this work, and what makes it important, will only encourage pride and productivity.

- **I UNDERSTAND THE ORGANIZATIONAL NORMS AND VOCABULARY OF THIS ORGANIZATION.** Investing time in helping externals understand the organization's culture and values is obvious. As the Driscoll's example indicates, it is important that external resources understand the context of the organization, and align its way of working with the organization's culture and way of working. And it is of obvious and immediate benefit to know the vocabulary of the organization and its industry or sector. Knowing the lingo of the organization confers immediate respect; after all, learning the language of the business and the abbreviations that are important is itself an act of respect.

- **I KNOW WHOM I NEED TO MEET, INVOLVE, AND SUPPORT.** The most valuable single outcome of a good onboarding orientation is a map of the organization and the key relationships that will affect advisory or project success. We suggest two categories of individuals: those who have the authority to say yes, and those who can muster a filibuster and, therefore, have the influence to say no. Relationships with both are essential and need to be cultivated.

Sponsorship

Sponsorship is critical to getting any external talent initiative off to a good start. Many of the executives in our study also describe the level of executive sponsorship as appropriate for the project or initiative and supportive of success. But interestingly, slightly more than half of the

FIGURE 4-4

Effectiveness of executive sponsorship for external talent

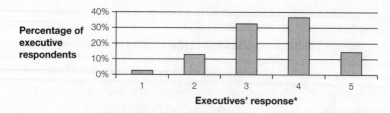

Source: Pilot study by RBL Group.

*Responses from the RBL pilot survey of 200 executives answering the question "How well do we ensure that sponsorship for external resources is at the right level for the work to succeed?" on a scale of 1 to 5, where 1 = not very effectively, 3 = neutral, and 5 = very effectively.

executives who responded to the question "How well do we ensure that sponsorship for external resources is at the right level for the work to succeed?" gave a rating at or below neutral (figure 4-4). When the level of sponsorship is inconsistent with the requirements for success, the work of the external resource is really an expensive crap shoot—not a good start for an important undertaking.

Anticipate and Address Potential Problems Up Front

Because even the best-considered activities don't go exactly as planned, it's important to anticipate potential problems when sourcing agile talent. Our survey data is enlightening in this area. Again, we find a nearly normal distribution of executives' answers to the question "How well do you anticipate problems and address them up front?" The good news is this: more organizations do anticipate potential problems in successfully completing the work and are addressing these issues up front. About a quarter of leaders are clear that they and their organizations

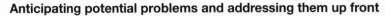

FIGURE 4-5

Anticipating potential problems and addressing them up front

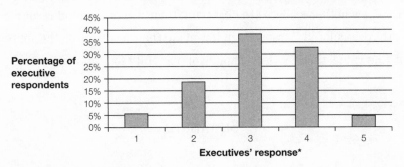

Source: Pilot study by RBL Group.

*Responses from the RBL pilot survey of 200 executives answering the question "How well do you antici-
pate problems and address them up front?" on a scale of 1 to 5, where 1 = not very effectively, 3 = neutral,
and 5 = very effectively.

could do a better job of working with external resources to identify
potential problems likely to arise in completing the assignment (col-
umns 1 and 2 in figure 4-5).

Communicate, Communicate

Finally, we asked executives about the frequency and timeliness of
ongoing communication with external agile talent. Here we see a distribution similar to the responses to other questions: around 20 percent
believe that their organization must improve in keeping agile talent
informed and up-to-date.

All these findings provide an interesting perspective. The combined responses suggest something other than a neutrality in how they
evaluate their organization; it implies a *satisficing*—"good enough"—
orientation by our executive respondents—they are neither pleased nor
displeased in general.

Given the very well established data on the effectiveness of change initiatives—70 percent of change initiatives are unsuccessful—we wonder whether leaders are observing their use of external resources with rose-colored glasses. Even if we take their feedback on the survey at face value, there is clearly ample opportunity for improvement.

Summary

In this chapter, we've described the opportunities that top companies have to create a different and more inclusive approach to the attraction, integration, and engagement of external agile talent as well as internal staff. This approach can make an important difference in the motivation, productivity, and performance of external experts. In the next chapter, we discuss the importance of aligning the skills and developmental maturity of both internal and external professionals, and how they create strong systems of collaboration.

5

Ensuring Professional Excellence

Growing Talent That You Don't Even Own

We have examined the importance of positioning the organization to better attract, welcome, and onboard agile talent. An employer branding approach enables organizations to appeal on a more targeted basis to needed external (and internal) resources. Because brand is a contract, not an advertisement, leaders must make the brand real by assessing the situation, defining needs for change, and reducing or closing the gap between what the employer brand offers and what it actually delivers.

From discussions with executives across industries, we also know that creating an environment that addresses the work and career interests of external experts is not often a priority for many organizations despite their dependence on externals. Our findings show that over half of executives see at least some potential for improvement. And, without doubt, a targeted employer brand, robust orientation and onboarding, and ongoing information sharing create a more productive environment for external talent. When leaders thoughtfully invest in building stronger connections with their external experts, they increase the likelihood that externals will do their best work and that the organization will continue to attract the skill it needs to achieve its vision and strategy.

In this chapter, we review how smart leaders ensure that their organization has the right mix of internal and external resources and that external experts have the required interpersonal skills and strategic perspective to successfully collaborate with internal colleagues. We consider three questions on this issue:

1. In addition to technical or functional expertise, are there other criteria important to building the right internal-external relationships?

2. How important are team skills and a bias to collaborate?

3. What is the role and importance of interpersonal competence or career maturity?

From Introduction to Contribution

The framework that best describes the set of skills and behavioral competencies external experts need to thrive is called the *career stages of performance*. Researchers Gene Dalton and Paul Thompson of Harvard Business School and, subsequently, the Brigham Young University Marriott School of Management, developed the stages framework.[1] Their work was based originally on research with R&D and engineering organizations, and was later extended by other researchers including us.[2] We were fortunate to work closely with Professors Dalton and

TABLE 5-1

Career stages of performance

Stage	How the individual contributes to the organization at this stage
Stage 1: Helper/learner	Earning trust and learning the work and the organization's culture
Stage 2: Independent contributor/ specialist	Demonstrating credibility and expertise
Stage 3: Mentor/coach	Contributing through and developing others; coordinating work between teams
Stage 4: Sponsor/strategist	Shaping or influencing organizational direction

Thompson for many years at a former consultancy, The Novations Group. Their work has greatly influenced our approach.

Dalton and Thompson's concept of career development departs from descriptions of expertise that emphasize technical depth. Dalton and Thompson found that career high performers moved through a series of four distinct stages of development (table 5-1). And as these high performers moved from one stage to the next, they were challenged to let go of the behaviors that previously made them successful, to pick up the new skills and perspective needed at the next stage.

Stage 1: Earning Trust, and Helping and Learning

People in stage 1 are apprentices, and high performers at this stage *help and learn and earn trust*. The work of stage 1 is learning the ropes and developing the technical reputation, cultural insight, and relationships necessary to do the right job in the right way with the right colleagues. Table 5-2 summarizes the work of stage 1 professionals.

A willing acceptance of supervision is key to success in stage 1. The individual is unproven and lacks organizational status credentials. As an apprentice, the individual will be closely monitored until the person

TABLE 5-2

What high performers in stage 1 do

- Work under close supervision
- Willingly accept direction; acknowledge lack of status and experience
- Cooperate with others as part of a team
- Earn the trust of colleagues by delivering on the basics
- Exercise "directed" creativity and initiative
- Perform well under pressure; deliver within time and budget constraints
- Learn the culture: "how we work here"

can manage his or her own work and has formed effective working relationships. Successful stage 1 professionals accept these limits and work through them.

Cultural savvy is a second critical factor, and the best performers at this stage demonstrate cultural aptitude. Every organization has its own unique way of doing things. Stage 1 professionals are expected to understand the values and norms of the organization and operate accordingly.

Creativity and initiative are important at stage 1, but until professionals demonstrate technical skill and build trusting relationships, they lack the standing to credibly recommend a better way.

At all career stages, but particularly at stage 1, mentors play a crucial role. A good mentor opens doors, makes introductions, provides practical counsel, and offers informed career guidance. Smart stage 1 professionals, and in fact professionals at all stages, recognize that reciprocity is core to any mutually satisfying relationship and certainly a mentoring relationship. We explore the topic of mentorship later in the book.

Both of us had early mentors who significantly influenced our work while we were at Exxon. Jon worked extensively with Herb Shepherd, a "father" of organization development and a cofounder of the National Training Laboratories in the United States. Shepherd taught Jon how to work with executives and to be patient in the change management process. Both of us were fortunate to have Thompson—an external—as a mentor while at Exxon.

Mentors like Shepherd and Thompson provide a mirror of reality for young (and not-so-young) knowledge workers who, in turn, work hard to show the mentor that they have what it takes to succeed. This reciprocity for both people involved in the relationship is a key to success. The apprentice learns from a more experienced and wiser professional while the mentor gets a bright, hardworking apprentice to get things done.

How long can an individual remain in stage 1? Unfortunately, some individuals never leave this stage; they do not progress technically, do not establish professional credibility, and continue to seek direction.

Stage 2: Contributing Independently

Stage 2 of professional development is the stage of the "arrived" technical or functional professional. The individual has reached technical maturity and enjoys acknowledged expertise. But while technical mojo is absolutely necessary for this stage of high performers, it is not sufficient. The professional must have the credibility and relationships to be recognized as an expert and sought out for his or her expertise. Dalton and Thompson describe the transition from apprentice to specialist as a renegotiation of the managerial relationship, from close supervision to broad navigational guidance. At stage 2, individuals are expected to demonstrate the technical expertise needed to solve difficult problems, the felt accountability to meet commitments, the resourcefulness to overcome obstacles, and the trust of colleagues inside and outside the organization. Table 5-3 summarizes the skills of stage 2 professionals.

Ambitious stage 2 employees actively seek ways to distinguish themselves as contributors. At this stage, professionals feel the competing

TABLE 5-3

What high performers in stage 2 do

- Work independently and produce significant results
- Establish credibility in a specific technical or functional area of expertise
- Renegotiate their supervisory relationship, shifting from close task direction to broad guidance
- Develop a reputation for work quality, reliability, and meeting commitments
- Demonstrate resourcefulness in solving problems or overcoming obstacles
- Seek and willingly accept personal accountability for results
- Build strong collegial relationships

tugs of competition and cooperation; stage 2 people must develop the team skills to work with and influence others. Some years ago, research by the People Operations team at Google put to bed the myth of the iconic expert who waits in the laboratory for difficult challenges and heroically solves them. Expertise is as much about outreach and initiative as it is about response.

Many experts are inclined to remain in stage 2. We call the most successful among them *super stage 2s*. Maintaining your status as stage 2 is not an easy path, requiring an expert to stay on top of the technology advances over time. This may be a greater challenge in some technical and functional areas than in others. Some years ago, Tom Jones, an IEEE fellow and the president of the University of South Carolina, estimated the half-life of an engineering degree to be around a decade; he further postulated that over a forty-year career, a typical engineer would need to spend ninety-six hundred hours to remain current. Ninety-six hundred hours is approximately twice the number of hours needed for the original degree.[3] No wonder that while super stage 2s are highly valued and often highly compensated, they are fairly rare. Functions evolve, technologies change, and recent graduates are often seen as offering technical know-how that is cheaper and more current.

Ultimately, the performance of stage 2 professional is limited by two factors. The first is their individual skill or expertise. Anders Ericcson and his coauthors were correct in citing the multi-thousand-hour rule, asserting that expertise is about practice and experience.[4] The second factor is time. Regardless of how technically and interpersonally outstanding the individuals may be, experts who want to increase their productivity, status, and responsibility must figure out how to increase their contribution beyond what they can individually accomplish. That is the challenge that professionals overcome in stage 3.

Stage 3: Contributing Through Others

The key to contributing beyond your personal limits is the ability to leverage the efforts of others. This is the stage 3 challenge; at this stage, experts are expected to contribute through others. The most obvious way to do so is as a formal manager. However, there are other ways for high performers to deliver a strong stage 3 performance.

What defines effective stage 3 professionals? First, they must remain up-to-date in their technical field. Over time, breadth compensates for depth: it enables the experts to see and share the bigger picture of the technology and make the right connections between various technologies, as well as between technical and business needs. Stage 3 professionals are, in short, integrators and optimizers.[5] Table 5-4 outlines the competences of this group of professionals.

TABLE 5-4

What high performers in stage 3 do

- Remain up-to-date technically
- Broaden their perspective and skills, helping others see the bigger picture
- Support others through ideas, knowledge, and insight
- Develop junior colleagues as a formal manager, an idea or project leader, or an informal mentor
- Build a strong internal and external network
- Effectively represent the team or organization when interacting with other internal or external groups

Stage 3 high performers are networkers and relationship builders: they build and maintain a strong network to get things done and keep in touch. Even more importantly, high-performing stage 3s are coaches and talent developers. Mentorship of less experienced colleagues is a hallmark of stage 3.

Stage 4: Shaping Organization Direction

The transition from stage 2 to 3 challenges individuals to break free of the limits of individual contribution. Stage 4 represents an equally significant shift: strategic guidance or influence. We think of stage 4 high performers as shaping organization direction. Primarily, this level of professional development requires an outside-in perspective, an informed point of view about the changing strategic needs of the larger organization and the ability to communicate this point of view clearly, succinctly, and persuasively (table 5-5).

While these skills might seem more manager oriented than technical, typically we see many technical stage 4 contributors especially in technology-oriented organizations. A former chief geologist of a major oil company and now a senior technical leader and certainly a stage 4, describes his role this way: "My job is to ensure that our company has the tools, talent, and culture to find significant oil and gas reserves."

TABLE 5-5

What high performers in stage 4 do

- Provide strategic focus to the organization
- Influence important organizational decisions and actions
- Lead change in how the organization operates: systems, processes, and practices
- Build organizational capability to align with strategic organizational goals
- Exercise power (formal and informal) for the benefit of the organization: make the tough decisions
- Sponsor promising individuals; test and prepare them for significant roles in future
- Represent the enterprise to key stakeholders

The preceding discussion of stage 4 in technical fields points out a critical skill of the high-performing stage 4. Whether the position is managerial or not, the role calls for solid leadership skills. That means a vision for the future, shifting from trying to influence to taking accountability for power, and knowing how to drive the actions that produce real change.

In our leadership pipeline audits, we sometimes find a business without any stage 4 leaders. Under these circumstances, the entire organization downshifts its performance. This happens because no one is responsible to set direction or provide resources to important projects. Stage 4 leaders, whether they are managerial or technical, are key to setting the vision and providing the infrastructure under which everything else must flow. When there is confusion, there is lack of accountability and a natural tendency to mediocrity. Tough choices and trade-offs must be made, and when they are not, the consequence is poor performance.

What Drives Development

One of the most interesting findings from the career stages research is the lack of gender or age as a critical determinant of stage. Women were slightly less represented in stages 3 and 4 but not much, and the difference continues to decrease. And age just doesn't seem to be a factor, as table 5-6 suggests. Moreover, stage development has little or nothing

TABLE 5-6

Average age of individuals by career stage

Career stage	Average age
Stage 1: Helper/learner	38
Stage 2: Independent contributor/specialist	38
Stage 3: Coach/mentor	39
Stage 4: Sponsor/strategist	41

Source: Jon Younger and Kurt Sandholtz, "Helping R&D Professionals Build Successful Careers," *Research and Technology Management* 60, no. 6 (November–December 1997).

FIGURE 5-1

The relationship between individuals' career stage and their perceived contribution

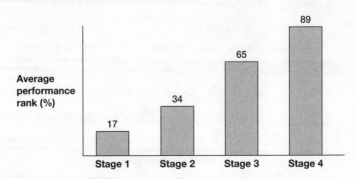

Sources: Gene W. Dalton and Paul H. Thompson, *Novations: Strategies for Career Management* (Glenview, IL: Scott Foresman, 1986); Jon Younger and Kurt Sandholtz, "Helping R&D Professionals Build Successful Careers," *Research Technology Management* 40, no. 6 (November–December 1997).

Note: Briefly, stage 1 is roughly equivalent to an apprentice level; stage 2, an independent contributor or specialist; stage 3, a mentor or coach; stage 4, a sponsor or director.

to do with the prestige of the universities attended, specific area of specialization, or degree. What does matter is how the individuals are managed and the opportunities offered them to grow and develop.[6]

Is there a relationship between career stage and performance relative to peers? The answer is an unequivocal yes. In an IRI reported study we conducted several years ago, managers in a wide variety of technical organizations were asked to rate the performance value of their subordinates; employees were separately evaluated by stage. The data was clear (figure 5-1).[7]

How the Career Stages Help Leaders Find and Support Agile Talent

The career-stages model offers an interesting and useful way of thinking about technical experts and expertise. It suggests a number of very specific ways that leaders can improve the selection and performance of external experts.

Not Just Technical

The clear message of the stages is that technical expertise, while obviously necessary, is not sufficient. Instead, we suggest a broader way of thinking about the requirements for success for external agile talent. In our view, agile talent has the technical skill, credibility, reliability, and relationship skills to be successful. These individuals are the people whom others want to call on for help when technical skill is required.

Both the executives and technical professionals we have interviewed and taught made this point repeatedly. Technical and functional experts must be more than expert at their craft. They must be good at working with the people who will implement their products, analyses, or recommendations, and these experts must have a strong-enough understanding of the organization's culture and norms to operate in an informed and respectful way. If they cannot meet these requirements, they will not be successful, however academically brilliant they might be. This is the reason why two equivalently technically talented individuals may have quite different career and contribution trajectories. It is also why some individuals never choose to develop beyond stage 1, or stall out in stage 2.

The career-stages research debunks the threadbare view of the expert as technical savant—the iconic scientist locked in a lab, unable to work effectively with others, brilliant but arrogant and brusque. Instead, the research findings offer a more helpful view: stage 2 demonstrates expertise and the ability to cooperate with colleagues; stage 3 shifts from the heroic individual expert to the coach and mentor who contributes through others; and, finally, stage 4 becomes the strategist and sponsor, influencing and shaping organizational direction.

Teaching and Using the Career Stages

An obvious first application of the career-stages approach to agile talent through cloud resourcing is to communicate and teach the approach as a tool in identifying resource needs and evaluating internal and external expert resources. Organizations like Exxon Mobil, Intel, Chevron, McKesson, and other leading global organizations have found career stages a helpful and easily understood framework for assessing the developmental stage of individuals and the mix of stages in a team or organization.

Match the Work and Stage

A second important application of the career-stage framework is enabling leaders to more rigorously determine the career stage required of external talents, and specifying the tasks or responsibilities to assign them. For example, a biotechnology manager who needs to add a contract researcher to his or her team traditionally describes the skills and experiences in terms of technical qualifications and work experience. Knowing which career stage the manager expects a contractor to fill adds additional precision to these specifications and focuses the search and credentials needed. What is the career stage role that this individual expected to play—stage 2, 3, or 4? Job and experience requirements would be more clearly defined. Use tool 5-1 for a simple approach to assessing the career stage of the individual and the job you hope to fill with agile talent.

We recommend a three-step diagnosis for identifying an individual's career stage:

1. **WHICH STAGE BEST REPRESENTS THE INDIVIDUAL'S BEHAVIOR?** First, identify which career stages provides the closest overall description of how the individual performs; the role the person adopts in relationships with colleagues, subordinates, and his or her supervisor; and the person's competence and effectiveness in working with others. In this first step, ignore the individual's formal role and position.

TOOL 5-1

Assessing the career stage of an individual or a job

Use this tool to compare the qualifications of each of the four career stages, and then decide where the individual you are assessing fits. You can also do the same thing for the job you are hoping to fill with agile talent.

Stage 1: Earn trust	Stage 2: Contribute independently
• Work under close supervision • Willingly accept direction; acknowledge lack of status and experience • Cooperate with others as part of a team • Earn the trust of colleagues by delivering on the basics • Exercise "directed" creativity and initiative • Perform well under pressure; deliver within time and budget constraints • Learn the culture: "how we work here"	• Work independently and produce significant results • Renegotiate the supervisory relationship, shifting from close task direction to broad guidance • Develop credibility and a reputation for expertise, reliability, and accomplishment • Demonstrate resourcefulness in solving problems or overcoming obstacles • Seek and willingly accept personal accountability for results • Build strong collegial relationships
Stage 3: **Leverage others**	**Stage 4:** **Shape organization's direction**
• Remain up-to-date technically • Broaden perspective and skills, helping others see the bigger picture • Support others through ideas, knowledge, and insight • Develop junior colleagues as a formal manager, an idea or project leader, or an informal mentor • Build a strong internal and external network • Effectively represent the team or organization when interacting with other internal or external groups	• Provide strategic focus to the organization • Influence important organizational decisions and actions • Lead change in how the organization operates: systems, processes, and practices • Build organizational capability to perform and achieve • Exercise power (formal and informal) for the benefit of the organization: make the tough decisions • Sponsor promising individuals; test and prepare them for significant roles in future • Represent the enterprise to key stakeholders

Realistically, many managers operate in stage 2 despite their role as a leader and mentor, and many nonmanagers provide coaching and mentorship consistent with stage 3. It is helpful to get multiple views on the individual's career stage. Different colleagues, with different perspectives, may experience the person's work in varied ways.

2. **IS THE INDIVIDUAL IN TRANSITION FROM ONE STAGE TO THE NEXT?** The career stages is a progressive rather than a prescriptive model; more often than not, individuals are in transition from one career stage to the next. This is important. If the individual is in transit, with one foot in stage 2 and another in stage 3, the role he or she plays will differ from an individual who is more fully in one stage or another. This behavior needs to be recognized. The tasks the person is assigned, whether he or she is an internal or an external resource, should reflect the transition the individual is making.

3. **WHAT, IF ANY, ORGANIZATIONAL AND CONTEXTUAL FACTORS MAY BE AFFECTING THE INDIVIDUAL'S CAREER-STAGE PERFORMANCE?** Particularly when working with external talent, it is important to understand any extrinsic and contextual factors that may influence their performance. Organizational factors include how the individual is used, the role he or she is given, the way the person is managed, and the way that the work is communicated to others with whom the individual must work. For example, if the individual's work director is an insecure stage 2, the supervisor is more likely to manage with a heavy hand. If internal team members are far more senior in career stage, they may discount the ability of the external resource to contribute; if they are far less senior in stage terms, it will be difficult for any real collaboration to occur.

External factors may also play a role. Many individuals currently face the challenge of a young family or aging parents; both situations typically make significant demands on the individual's time. Consequently, an individual may choose to take on a role typical of a lower career stage, making less of a demand on time and travel, in order to meet family requirements.

Recommendations for implementing a career-stages approach:

1. **START WITH THE ORGANIZATION FIRST**. For example, if Twitter is interested in attracting a senior software developer on a short contract basis, what does "senior" mean? We suggest it means more, or should mean more, than technical experience. Whether explicit or implicit, specifications should address the other critical success factors of a senior software developer. The career-stages approach provides an easily understood and data-based reference point.

2. **ASSESS THE STAGE OF INDIVIDUALS WHO MAY DO THE TASK**. As we suggested above, assessing the stage of individuals is obviously important. However, when considering external agile talent, leaders may have difficulty identifying a person's career stage during a brief interview. But stepping outside the bound-aries of the interview will help. Speak with prior client organiza-tions or colleagues who have worked with the individual in the past. As described above, share a summary of the career stages, and ask your associates which stage most closely resembles the individual's way of working. Keep in mind that career stage is not a personality test; it is a description of how individuals go about their work at different stages of development.

3. **DETERMINE THE FIT**. After assessing the career stage of the work to be done and the career stages of the individuals who

are being considered for the project or consulting contract, identify which individual is the best fit for the work and the group. It is at this stage that the details of experience and personality come into play.

Align Peer and Supervisory Relationships

It is particularly important to ensure that there is not too great a gulf between internal and external experts working together, and especially when you are selecting internal project managers of external experts. Obviously, it wouldn't do to have a stage 2 internal project leader managing a stage 3 or 4 external expert—but such an arrangement happens too often and is often disastrous. The flip side is equally likely to end in difficulty. A very senior project leader managing a junior external resource or team is likely to be frustrated by the quality and speed of progress. The findings of the career-stage research are clear with respect to internal project management of high-performing external experts: the internal project manager must be operating at stage 3 or higher or must be making clear, fast strides toward stage 3. If they are stage 2, the competitive tendency of that stage may reduce the performance of external talents. For example, we collaborated with a major investment bank to help them build a plan for accelerated leader development. It was a timely project that was linked to strategy business goals, and its success was a priority for senior management. Yet, a mismatch in career stage hurt its contribution. The bank appointed an ambitious young stage 2 professional to work with and support the consulting team. Instead, he saw the team as competition and insisted on controlling all communication between the consulting team and the organization. This created significant delays in completing the project, and it ultimately led to the company abandoning the project.

Google rediscovered the career-stages research in its internal study of "good" and "bad" managerial behaviors. Unsurprising for those of us who are familiar with the career-stages literature, but evidently an epiphany for the Google HR team, is the list of behaviors compiled by Google HR and based on extensive analytics (table 5-7). The left side of the table is a full-on description of stage 3.[8]

Career Stage Is Not the Same as Hierarchy

One of the common concerns about the four stages is to think of it in terms of the organization's hierarchy. There is some truth to this as expectations change for how someone works as he or she spends time in an organization. For example, if someone is considered a high performer at age twenty-five but continues to work the same way at age thirty-five, managers ask what is wrong. In addition, there is no need to try to limit the number of stage 3 contributors. Stage 3 roles don't need formal leadership positions. They can be technical people who have changed

TABLE 5-7

Google's good boss, bad boss analysis

Good managerial behaviors	Three pitfalls of managers
• Be a good coach	• Having difficulty dealing with making changes to the team
• Empower your team; don't micromanage	
• Express interest in team members' success and well-being	• Lacking a consistent approach to performance management and careering development
• Don't be a wimp; be productive and results-oriented	• Spending too little time managing and communicating
• Be a good communicator, and listen to your team	
• Help your employees with career development	
• Have a clear vision and strategy for the team	
• Have technical skills so you can help advise the team	

Source: Adam Bryant, "Google's quest to build a better boss," *New York Times*, March 12, 2011, http://www.nytimes.com/2011/03/13/business/13hire.html.

the nature of their contribution. Think of a business partner in IT, HR, or finance. The person assigned to the business partner role could be in stage 1, 2, or 3. As a stage 1 business partner, he or she tends to execute projects under the direction of another person. As a stage 3 business partner, the individual translates business needs into projects for his or her function. In every organization for which we have done work on this issue, there are never enough stage 3 people. Stage 3 professionals are usually the key to successful initiatives because the stage 3s who are not managers are closer to the technical work and the customer and are able to integrate the work of others to achieve effective outcomes.

Define the Optimal Mix at a Team Level

The old expression "The magic is in the mix" certainly fits the definition of the optimal distribution of career stages on a team. IBM and Microsoft are two of many technical organizations that regularly bring together mixed teams of internal software developers and external agile talent to a development team. What mix of career stages delivers the expertise required to achieve the goals of the organization?

It turns out that IBM looked carefully at this issue several years ago. Research leadership noticed that some software development teams dubbed "super teams" were many times more productive than others as measured by schedule, cost, and numbers of people. The team studied the difference between super teams and other teams.

They discovered that the greatest differentiator was whether the team was staffed according to career-stages concepts. The most successful teams had the right mix of stage 1 through 4 experts at each stage of a project, operating with specific roles in mind for each stage (figure 5-2).

By contrast, poorer-performing project teams were under-resourced in stages 3 and 4 and typically attempted to close the performance gap

FIGURE 5-2

IBM super project teams: the right mix of career stages and roles

Stage 1 or 2: Do the work	+	Stage 3: Manage, coach, and coordinate	+	Stage 4: Champion, resource, and protect

by bringing on additional stage 1 and 2 professionals at critical points in time. This approach generally increased both costs and schedule slips.[9]

Closing the Gap

Determining the right mix of career stages for your agile talent is a five-step process. Tool 5-2 provides a simple framework of the career stages. It describes the role played in each stage, the individual's relationship to colleagues, what the role demands, and the performance leverage (how individuals at each stage deliver value).

With this tool in hand, take the following steps:

1. Review the career stages. After getting an overview, you might find it helpful to identify individuals who are well known and who are good representatives of different stages. Giving individuals models to relate to, that make the career stages real, is a useful first step.

2. Sort your current resources—both internal and external, on contract or advising—by career stage. For those moving between stages, indicate whether they have progressed sufficiently to perform at the higher stage.

3. Define your organization's optimal mix by career stage today and a year or two ahead: what mix of stages is required to do the work of the function or technical team or organization at a

TOOL 5-2

Determining the right mix of stages among externals and internals on your team

See the text for how to use this tool.

	Stage 1	Stage 2	Stage 3	Stage 4
Role	Helper and learner	Independent contributor	Contribute through others	Shape organizational direction
Relationship	Apprentice	Colleague and specialist	Manage, mentor, idea leader, or project lead	Sponsor and strategist
Role adjustments	Dependence	Autonomy and accountability	Assuming responsibility for others	Exercising power
Performance leverage	Support to others	Expertise	Integrate and optimize	Change leadership

high-performing level? And, based on this assessment, identify them. Defining these mixes also defines the gap between the "what is" and the "what should be."

4. Determine the plan to close the gap. Here is where the organization returns to the strategic resourcing matrix we described in chapter 3 and provided in figure 3-1. What mix of internal staff and agile talent will provide the organization with the greatest opportunity to improve effectiveness and efficiency? What are the opportunities and prerequisites for building, buying, or renting expertise?

5. Finally, take action to implement the plan. The actions broadly fit into three categories. First, where will a change in the resourcing mix enable the organization to take greater

advantage of agile resourcing? Use the strategic resourcing matrix from figure 3-1 to make this determination. Second, how should the composition of internal resources be modified to complement agile talent resourcing plans? For example, if project managers don't have stage 3 skills, how can the organization accelerate their development and competence to make the best use of contractors and other externals? Third, be clear and insistent about the stage mix of external resources needed to deliver the value required and put in place a process of performance review and feedback to ensure the requirements are met.

Summary

There are a variety of applications of the career stages; we have only reviewed a few in this chapter. The most fundamental is the help that the career-stages approach provides in answering the question "What do I need to do to be seen as a strong performer?" In a study we completed several years ago, only 43 percent of the technical professionals we polled could confidently respond positively to the question "I know what I need to do to be successful in this organization." A good working knowledge of the career stages by both managers and individuals increased this number to 80 percent.

We have examined how agile talent is best attracted, recruited, developed, and engaged, whether the experts are internal staff or external partners. In the next chapter, we look at practical methods of increasing the productivity of external agile talent, setting up and aligning responsibilities within the mixed team, and more fully engaging externals who are working in your organization.

6

Engaging and Collaborating with Your Talent

Supporting Your Teams of Internals and Externals

In an earlier chapter, we show that how external agile talent enters an organization affects the productivity and commitment of this talent. The time and effort taken to orient externals to the task, their understanding of the goals they must deliver, their introduction to the culture of the organization, and their first opportunities to meet internal colleagues with whom they will work—all these things matter. These elements have an outsized impact on the individuals' subsequent work performance and how it affects other people whom they collaborate with or support.

Researchers describe engagement in a number of ways, from "feelings of commitment to the workplace" to "the process by which an organization increases commitment and continuation of its employees to the achievement of superior results." Measures of engagement almost invariably involve survey-based methods in which the participants are asked to respond to statements such as these:

- "I am proud to work for this company."

- "I give 100 percent to the job."

- "I would recommend this organization to a friend."

- "The work is energizing and exciting."

- "I enjoy the challenges I find in my work."

- "I am committed to giving my best efforts to the job."

The impact of engagement on individual performance and motivation is very clear. Highly engaged people, according to Curt Coffman, coauthor of *First, Break All the Rules*, "want to know the desired expectations for their role so they can meet and exceed them. They're naturally curious . . . They perform at consistently high levels. They want to use their talents and strengths at work every day. They work with passion, and they have a visceral connection to the company. And they drive innovation and move their organization forward."[1]

Employees who are engaged perform better, are more likely to recommend the company to potential employees and customers, and demonstrate greater organizational loyalty. Moreover, a trend toward disengagement has been growing over the past several years. Gallup recently reported that only 13 percent of employees worldwide describe themselves as highly engaged, a decrease in percentage over the past decade. Almost two-thirds of employees are best described as *nonengaged*; they regard their organization in more neutral terms. The remaining people are *actively disengaged*, cynical about their organization and unwilling to give more than what is necessary to keep their job.[2]

External agile talent is no different from internal employees when it comes to engagement. Highly engaged external experts are more likely to contribute their best work. They are more willing to invest discretionary time on behalf of the organization and project. They are more likely to collaborate when working with other external experts and internal staff. And it is well established that engagement is correlated positively with organizational performance.

Give External Resources a VOI^{2}C^{2}E

What drives engagement? In our teaching and consulting work, we use a framework for engagement we call VOI^{2}C^{2}E, which was first developed by RBL and our colleague Dave Ulrich in work for General Electric's Work-Out initiative. The framework describes seven key drivers of engagement:

- **VISION**: Leaders have a clear sense of the future of the organization, which engages hearts and minds and creates pride among the people who work there. People know, understand, and support the vision of the organization and their contribution to the vision. The work is meaningful and important, not just a job.

- **OPPORTUNITY**: The work provides a chance to grow both personally and professionally. Development is encouraged and supported; expertise is prized and reinforced through continuing education, work responsibilities, and relationships.

- **IMPACT**: The work itself makes a difference and has meaning and importance. People see the tangible result of their contribution to the organization.

- **INCENTIVES**: Strong performance is expected, recognized, and rewarded both financially and with opportunity to grow professionally.

- **COMMUNICATION**: People feel well informed about current events affecting their work, their colleagues, and the organization overall. Information is shared openly and appropriately.

- **COMMUNITY**: People feel part of a team where individuals are focused on the same goals and are supportive of one another in accomplishing shared tasks.

- **EMPOWERMENT**: People feel supported when they take a reasonable risk; they feel that they have latitude to act and take initiative when it is important and necessary to do so.[3]

How well does your organization provide employees with a VOI^2C^2E? Rate your organization on each of the seven elements, as it would feel to internal employees.

Now, rate your organization a second time, but this time, focus on agile talent rather than full-time, permanent employees. Are your responses similar for both the employees and the external talent, or do they diverge? Figure 6-1 provides an example: how internal members and the external agile talent of a leading pharmaceutical firm described their experience of engagement in the organization. As the figure indicates, the internal employees generally described themselves as more strongly engaged in most aspects of VOI^2C^2E than did the external experts, who were often working alongside the internal employees. In fact, the only area where externals described their experience as stronger was in incentives. In this area, the agile talent pointed out that the organization paid well, promptly, and without a good deal of administrative bureaucracy.

Not surprisingly, then, organizations generally devote less attention to the experiences of their agile talent. Realistically, the quality of engagement is largely not where it should be for either the permanent or the external workforce. However, the picture painted here is particularly bleak with respect to external agile talent. In the

FIGURE 6-1

VOI²C²E example: internal and external professionals' impressions of their level of engagement at a leading pharmaceutical company

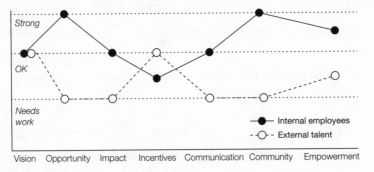

Note: VOI²C²E stands for seven key aspects of how talent is engaged with an organization: vision, opportunity, impact, incentives, communication, community, and empowerment.

typical corporation, the tactic of keeping agile talent engaged is at best an afterthought. This is a troublesome situation. Although leaders may think that agile talent need not feel engaged or may believe that the relationship is merely transactional, if executives want to get the most from their agile talent and the investment they've made in this resource, then they ignore these relationships at their peril. When a significant percentage of the total labor budget of an organization goes to external resources, it is shortsighted to think, as many executives are wont to do, "Your paycheck is your engagement."

Impediments to Engagement

Obligations in an external-internal relationship are not all one way, of course. A recent article by Avi Dan describes the frustrations of executives with external agile talent, specifically, with advertising agencies and their professionals.[4] The main categories of frustration won't be a surprise to leaders reading this chapter; the concerns for this type of external expert are generalizable:

- **GREATER ORGANIZATIONAL AND SERVICE ALIGNMENT**: "67% [of clients] see an opportunity to align client/agency teams better; almost half of the respondents, 47%, believe that training is necessary, while 41% say that clients need to do a better job of fighting silos at their end."[5]

- **MORE PROACTIVE**: "Agencies need to be become more proactive in experimenting with different business models. Today's agency models are constructed to suit the agencies, not the clients . . . They need to embrace measurement and integration as an intrinsic part of their offering if they want to be perceived as having a higher value by marketers."

- **MORE ACCOUNTABILITY FOR RESULTS**: "When asked what recent changes in marketing influenced them the most, 55% of clients pointed to growing demands for 'accountability' as the main factor . . . Yet, accountability is their main area of frustration with agencies—71% point to it as the area that agencies need to improve most."

- **SKILLS MUST CONTINUE TO IMPROVE**: "47% think that training is necessary . . . Another area in which agencies fall short of expectations are the skills required for delivering integrated communications."

Consultants and other agile talent also have a perspective on how organizations can be designed and operated to reinforce their productivity. In *Ivy Business Journal*, Gordon Perchthold and Jenny Sutton offer several recommendations:

- "[A] central point of accountability across the enterprise [responsible] for consultant [costs] and [assessment] of the value realized.

- "A clear statement of work; internal executive agreement on the problem to be solved, and the objective of the work.

- "Up-front agreement on the metrics used to assess project performance.

- "Executives, managers, and employees who will be working with consultants are educated on how to work with and manage consultants.

- "The company configures a project team of competent internal employees in consultation with the chosen consulting firm . . .

- "The company retains a strong role in project management . . . supplemented by the consulting firm's engagement manager . . .

- "Lessons learned by employees working on projects with consultants are captured, retained, and disseminated."[6]

Raising Agile Talent Engagement

What can organizations do to increase the level of engagement among their agile talent and, therefore, increase both the performance and the contribution of externals and their working relationships with internal counterparts? The seven VOI^{2}C^{2}E factors, beginning with vision, provide very helpful guidance.

Vision

External resources generally, and millennial externals in particular, want to do meaningful work that has an impact. Although the project or advisory role may focus on a part of a larger whole, external agile talent will be more engaged if leaders communicate the bigger picture of the work the externals are asked to do. Agile talent needs to know the contribution that the work will make to the organization and its customers or stakeholders. Readers may have heard the story of the bricklayer:

> A man walking along the road met three bricklayers. He asked them all the same question: "What are you doing?" The first bricklayer unhappily said, "I'm laying bricks." The second halfheartedly said, "I'm building a wall." The third enthusiastically proclaimed, "I'm building a temple."

People are motivated by important work, and external agile talent earns future clients and interesting assignments by doing important work these experts can talk about and by sharing information on the results they have achieved. Leaders who share the context of the work and the bigger picture will create greater engagement.

For example, in the past year, Baxter Healthcare spun off a new bioscience company called Baxalta. The vision of this new company is to contribute to medicines that help cure rare conditions in oncology, hematology, and immunology. Baxalta contracted with us at the RBL Group to help design an HR organization that is more fully aligned with its priorities. It's fascinating to see how excited the new leaders of Baxalta are about their mission and how they hope to develop new products that will make a difference to patients. This excitement becomes contagious when it is shared through communication and involvement. As externals, the team working with Baxalta feels more engaged in part because this is important and exciting work, but also because the organization's leaders take the time to include the external talent working with them.

FIGURE 6-2

Five important criteria in work design

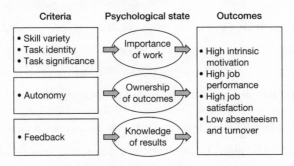

Source: Adapted from J. Richard Hackman and Greg R. Oldham, *The Job Diagnostic Survey: An Instrument for the Diagnosis of Jobs and Evaluation of Job Redesign Projects* (Arlington, VA: Office of Naval Research, 1974).

Opportunity

Some years ago, Dick Hackman and Greg Oldham of Yale University identified several factors that were at the heart of effective job design. Using what they called the "job diagnostic survey," they found that satisfying and influential jobs met five criteria (figure 6-2).[7]

Hackman and Oldham found that good work design—work that is productive and satisfying to individuals—is the result of attention to these five factors:

- **SKILL VARIETY:** The work requires a range of activities, requiring the individual to develop and utilize a variety of skills and talents. People experience more meaningfulness when work requires different skills and abilities than when work is monotonous and routine.

- **TASK IDENTITY:** The work requires the person to complete a work product rather than just being responsible for one part of an outcome. People experience more meaningfulness when they are involved in a entire process rather than just a part of it.

- **TASK SIGNIFICANCE:** The work has impact, influencing colleagues, customers, or the larger organization. People feel more meaningfulness when the work improves the well-being of others instead of having a limited impact on anyone else.

- **AUTONOMY:** The work provides the employee with significant discretion to plan out the work and determine how to best accomplish the task. For jobs with a high level of autonomy, the outcomes of the work depend on the workers' own efforts, initiatives, and decisions rather than the direction of a manager or a standard operating procedure. In high-autonomy jobs, people experience greater personal responsibility for success and failure.

- **FEEDBACK:** The worker is provided with specific information about work performance. When workers receive clear, actionable feedback, they are better able to improve their productivity.

These five criteria provide a helpful way to assess both internal full-time work assignments and, of course, the project assignments or other roles of external agile talent. A simple but potentially powerful application of these criteria is to use them to assess and improve the work plan for future talent. How could leaders, for example, build in more regular and targeted feedback? We recommend that external experts and internal staffs assess their progress on the five criteria as a way to incorporate multiple views and to target areas for improvement.

Impact

Two aspects of impact will drive higher levels of engagement. The first is feedback about the performance of the work. External experts want

TABLE 6-1

Typical after-action review meeting agenda

1. Review the purpose of the after-action review and ground rules for discussion.
2. Consider the goal: what outcome was intended?
3. Consider the result: what actually happened?
4. Review the positive aspects: what went well, and why?
5. Discuss improvements to make: what can be improved for the future, and how should those improvements be made?
6. Allow for closing comments, and discuss what needs to be communicated to whom, and when.

to know how well their work has met the goals and has created value for the organization. We have already talked about the importance of performance feedback earlier in the book.

In addition to performance feedback, we encourage the use of *after-action review* and the involvement of external experts in the review. After-action review was created by the US armed forces as a way to maximize learning after a project is completed: What did we do right? What could we have done better? How effective was our planning, communication, and collaboration? A typical after-action review meeting lasts only a few hours and involves the key stakeholders of a project— internal staff members, external experts, customers or suppliers where appropriate, and other important participants. A representative after-action review agenda is shown in table 6-1.

Incentives

Research on motivation describes two types of rewards: intrinsic and extrinsic. Intrinsic rewards are those a person generates in the course of doing the work. They may reflect appreciation of the task and its challenge, the opportunity to learn new skills, the chance to work with interesting colleagues, or the location of the work itself. Extrinsic rewards are those outside the work itself, such as pay, perquisites, and other benefits.

The majority of recommendations we've made so far in this book are ways to increase the intrinsic rewards an external expert may experience working with an organization: the work itself is a source of reward when the topic is interesting or enjoyable, when there is opportunity to develop new skills or expertise, or when the person has the chance to work with interesting, collaborative colleagues.

In addition to this source of reward, other sources of extrinsic reward may be more specifically relevant to the external agile talent. A simple example is to invite externals to participate in presentations to executives of the organization. We have seen this sort of extrinsic reward in our own work. For example, one of us was invited to the senior leadership team offsite of Savage Industries (a global supply-chain company), where an internal team of high-potential employees presented the recommendations for a business reorganization project on which we had jointly worked. In an explicit effort at engaging and thanking the internals and externals (and, hopefully, to add value at the meeting), Savage senior leaders invited the whole team to the meeting. Several of the internal staff have commented on how grateful they are to work for a company that does this. We feel the same. Another example is the opportunity to publish or present to colleagues the key findings of a project. All of these examples offer opportunities to increase the incentive for an expert to do his or her best work. Finding ways to motivate agile talent beyond the paycheck will only help bind the individuals or team to the organization's best interests.

Communication

We have written at length about the importance of communication. Four directions of communication are important to external agile talent and the relationship between this talent and internal colleagues.

Engaging agile talent through communication means being attentive to all directions of communication:

- **UP**: While completing the work, do externals feel that they have the opportunity to provide feedback to more-senior leaders if it is needed and as it is needed?

- **DOWN**: Does the external agile talent have the opportunity to hear and understand the executive perspective on the project and its contribution? Are these externals also told about internal and outside events that may affect the project?

- **ACROSS**: Do external partners have the opportunity to coordinate their work with other external experts or internal staff working on similar or overlapping projects in other parts of the organization?

- **OUT**: Does the agile talent have the opportunity to share the work and its impact with outside audiences?

Having identified these four directions of communication, leaders might assess how well they support the engagement of external experts and their motivation to do their best work, with the assessment tool 6-1. Using this simple set of questions, which should be completed by both internal staff working with external experts, and the external experts themselves, the organization is likely to find practical ways to increase engagement.

Community

We have talked previously about involving external agile talent in the stream of organizational activity as a way of increasing engagement. Building collaborative teams is an obvious way to increase teamwork

TOOL 6-1

How well does your organization's communications support agile talent?

Rate your organization on a scale of 1 to 5, where 1 = not well, and 5 = very well.

Direction of communication	Rating
1. How well do we use *upward* communication—opportunities for feedback to executives—to engage the external experts with whom we work?	
2. How well do we use *downward* communication—communication from executives—to engage the external experts with whom we work?	
3. How well do we use *lateral* communication—information from individuals in other units—to engage the external experts with whom we work?	
4. How well do we use *outward* communication—information from respected external sources—to engage the external experts with whom we work?	

and engagement. Jon Katzenbach and Douglas Smith, both authors and consultants, have conducted helpful research on the levels of teamwork within organizations. The research provides leaders with a way of assessing whether teams of internals and externals working together have the right level of cooperation. Katzenbach and Smith describe a hierarchy of teamwork as follows:

- **THE WORKING GROUP.** The members interact mainly to share information. There are no common purpose or performance goals that require mutual accountability. The focus is on individual performance. There is no significant, incremental performance need or opportunity that requires the group to become a team.

- **THE PSEUDO TEAM.** There is potential for significant gain here, but the team has not focused on collective performance. The members don't want to take the actions to become a team and don't see the value of common purpose or shared goals.

- **THE POTENTIAL TEAM.** The members are working hard to achieve a higher level of performance but do not fully share a clear purpose, goals, or a common approach. The greatest gain in performance comes from the shift from a potential team to a real team.

- **THE REAL TEAM.** Real teams are groups of people who share a common purpose, goals, and approach to work and who hold themselves mutually accountable for their results.

- **THE HIGH-PERFORMANCE TEAM.** High-performing teams have the characteristics of a real team, and its members are deeply committed to one another's success. These teams far outperform all other teams.[8]

Katzenbach and Smith's work provides a helpful, simple, and straightforward approach to assessing the level of teamwork and identifying the needs for improvement to increase the quality of performance and engagement. An approach we've developed and found helpful is a three-step teamwork gap analysis:

1. What level of teamwork is required for the project to be successful and for internal and external colleagues to experience real engagement?

2. What is the level of teamwork now? Why?

3. If the level of teamwork is below the requirement, what actions are most likely to quickly and meaningfully close the gap?

One of the benefits of this approach is the discovery that big improvements often follow from small changes. In work with Damco, the A.P. Moller-Maersk supply-chain division, an action learning project team meeting identified the simple importance of setting and keeping a regular meeting schedule. Doing so put the team on a path from pseudo team to potential team and, eventually, to real team status. The improved team created a new business that is now generating significant revenues.

Empowerment

The last factor in VOI^2C^2E is empowerment. This driver of engagement refers to a willingness to seek the best work of external resources, rather than hamstringing them with excessive direction about how to complete the task. Empowerment is particularly important whenever the career orientation of the agile talent is autonomy, but that's not the only case. External resources want to use and continue to develop their expertise; beyond being a source of pride and identification, it is their source of livelihood and reputation. When organizations overdirect the efforts of their agile talent, they are likely to get less than these experts' best work.

Who Is Minding the Store? Chief External Talent Officers

The role of chief learning or chief talent officer is now a common executive position in large global companies. The chief talent officer is responsible for managing the firm's employment brand and new-employee recruiting and development and is often involved in succession and executive compensation.

The problem with the role of this executive is that the position has ignored the growing importance and involvement of external agile talent. There are obvious differences between attracting, developing, and retaining internal "regular" employees and acting as a talent chief for external talent. Nevertheless, for organizations that are making an increased commitment to agile talent, the role of external talent leader is important. We are not aware of any companies currently employing a senior externally focused talent officer, although these roles are managed informally. Table 6-2 compares what internal and externally focused talent officers do.

In Silicon Valley, Ben Horowitz, one of the founders of venture capital firm Andreesen Horowitz, is known as something of a mentor for the next generation of internet entrepreneurs. Some years ago, as director of product development at LoudCloud, he wrote a now-famous memo titled "Good Product Manager, Bad Product Manager." The first paragraph illustrates Horowitz's views:

> Good product managers know the market, the product, the product line and the competition extremely well and operate from a strong basis of knowledge and confidence. A good product manager is the CEO of the product. A good product manager takes full responsibility and measures themselves in terms of the success of the product. They are responsible for right product/right time and all that entails. A good product manager knows the context going in (the company, our revenue funding, competition, etc.), and they take responsibility for devising and executing a winning plan (no excuses).[9]

This isn't a bad description of what we mean by the external talent manager (or, alternatively, the head of a corporate project management office). His or her job is to perform what Horowitz describes as good

TABLE 6-2

Internal versus external talent officers

Factor	Internal talent officer	External talent officer
Workforce plan	Identifies overall workforce needs according to company strategy	Identifies external expertise needs according to company strategy
Attracting and recruitment	Employment brand leader; builds strong relationships with potential employee pools	Knows the external marketplace; identifies external individuals and firms that meet the company's work and cultural alignment needs; builds strong relationships with external experts and firms
Onboarding	Ensures that new employees have an effective orientation and onboarding experience, are able to navigate the organization effectively, build important early relationships, and find a mentor	Works with the external firm to establish the right early relationships, especially the team members the officer is working with and the internal executive sponsor of the project
Development	Ensures that employees have the training they need to perform well	Ensures that employees are effective collaborators with external experts, and ensures that externals understand the culture of the organization and can operate effectively within it; communicates to both internals and externals that if they are unable to work effectively with the other group, they will be replaced
Assessment	Assesses the performance and potential of employees	Assesses the performance of the externals according to the scope of work on a collaborative basis; deeply involves internal colleagues and externals, and recommends whether the outside expert or firm should continue to work with the organization on future projects; also manages the companywide database of externals
Career management	Provides career management support to employees and guidance on the identification of high potentials for accelerated development	Is mindful of individual externals whom the company would like to hire as full-time employees, and builds those relationships.
Diversity	Ensures that the organization creates an environment of open communication, respect, and fairness among employees	Pays attention to how consultants are treated in the organization, and addresses situations proactively, before they become a problem

product management; in fact, the job responsibility of the external talent officer is to ensure that the organization does a rigorous job of selecting external expertise, creates the conditions for success, and challenges the organization to consistently learn from each project experience and from the overall trends. In short, the role we imagine is essentially a product manager of external relationships and resources.

Summary

In the past few chapters, we have examined the key elements of aligning an organization's cloud resourcing strategy and priorities with how well the organization is set up to engage agile talent and establish the conditions for these individuals or groups to do their best work. The alignment of organizational strategy with the cloud resourcing of agile talent starts with how outside experts are brought into the organization, welcomed, and oriented. How well the organization aligns internal staff relationships, builds systems of collaboration, and focuses time and effort on the engagement of part-time and contracted staff pays clear dividends in the results that engaged and motivated externals deliver. In the next chapter, we review the role of leaders in creating high-performing agile talent.

7

Leading Agile Talent

Understanding the Skills You Need
and How to Apply Them

As with success in meeting other strategic changes, the effective tapping of agile talent depends on the quality of leadership. Unless leaders embrace the opportunity for, and tactics of, greater talent agility and actively sponsor the shift, employees and lower-level managers are likely to be resistant. Where leaders do not take the actions needed to effectively implement agile talent, this talent will not deliver the benefits.

On a recent trip to Kyoto, one of us learned about a unique sixteenth-century security system at Nijo Castle. Called the *nightingale floor*, it was designed to "chirp" when walked upon, alerting the guards if an intruder was sneaking in.

With its defensive orientation, the nightingale floor is a fitting metaphor for how frequently leaders and organizations are inclined to see agile talent in us-versus-them terms. Rather than view agile talent as partners and a valued extension or reinforcement of internal capability, organizations too often view external talent with suspicion, or as a necessary but lamentable evil.

With this attitude, the organization is disadvantaged in multiple ways: disengaged agile talent wastes the time and effort of both the externals and the internal staff working with it or depending on it. The often-costly investment of working with external talent is suboptimized. The organization is inattentive to good counsel and best practices. And over time, the organization may develop a reputation for being poor clients or for establishing poor working relations with external talent. Such a reputation makes agile talent less engaged with the organization and consequently less effective. With less effective external resources, the organization feels less compelled to engage its outside talent, and a downward spiral of poor performance can ensue.

The Leadership Code

What are the skills required by the leaders of organizations seeking the benefits of agile talent and expanding their use of cloud resourcing? Our work in leadership development is helpful in this context. Faced with the incredible volume of information about leadership (over 475 million separate entries in a Google search), we honed in on the opinions of experts in the field who had earned a reputation for their work in leaders and leadership. In our discussions with them, we focused on two fundamental questions:

1. What percentage of effective leadership is described similarly across the range of leadership research and theories?

FIGURE 7-1

The leadership code: five foundational competencies

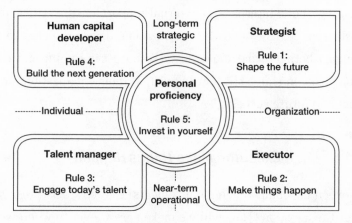

Source: Dave Ulrich, Norm Smallwood, and Kate Sweetman, *The Leadership Code: Five Rules to Lead By* (Boston: Harvard Business Review Press, 2008), 14.

2. If there are common skill sets that all leaders must master to be an effective leader, regardless of industry (or not-for-profit status), what are these skills?

Our study found that 60 to 70 percent of good leadership is similarly described by theorists and researchers. When asked to describe the 60 to 70 percent, the respondents showed an exceedingly high degree of convergence in concept, regardless of small differences in nuance and language. We call these basics the *leadership code*, which we examined in detail in *The Leadership Code: Five Rules to Lead By*.[1] Figure 7-1 presents a visual framework of the five rules of leadership constituting the code.

Strategist: Shape the Future

Strategists answer the question "Where are we going?" and ensure that the workforce—both internal and external—understands the goals of the organization, the workforce's contribution to those goals, and the importance of people's effort and performance to customers, investors and other stakeholders. Strategists envision the possibilities, define the strategy, build internal and external support, ensure critical inputs (investments, skills), build the organization, devise the change plan, and engage both internal and external resources in owning and achieving the goals. In short, strategists position their organization for both current and future success.

Executor: Make Things Happen

The executor competence complements the strategist: executors answer the question "How will we make sure we get to where we are going?" They translate strategy into a plan of action, make change happen, and ensure a high-performing culture that is consistent with the organization's goals, establishes accountability, supports innovation, and puts the right people together in the right teams with a clear focus. Leaders operating as executors establish the organizational and performance disciplines that convert plans into programs of action and that convert action into results.

Talent Manager: Engage Today's Talent

Effective leaders develop and engage talent: they identify the skills needed for high performance, and they encourage, develop, and motivate people—internal and external—to feel ownership for the organization's goals. Talent managers ensure that the competencies required for success are in place, accessible, and delivered effectively and cost- and time-efficiently. To engage people, talent managers appropriately deploy both technical and interpersonal skills and build enthusiasm through communication and involvement. As performance disciplinarians, talent managers are unafraid to take prompt action in response to poor performance, but they equally act as coaches and mentors, and investors in high performance.

Human Capital Developer: Build the Next Generation

Talent managers focus on current goals and challenges and the agile talent required to overcome these challenges. But industries change and a key task of effective leaders is to be thoughtfully aware of new performance requirements requiring new capabilities. For example, Uber senior leaders recognize that the next generation of their business is likely to involve a massively disruptive shift from driver to autonomous (or self-driving) taxis. Consequently, they established a relationship with Carnegie Mellon University's National Robotics Engineering Center, the same center that is providing innovative robotics technology to the US military.

Uber leaders provide a helpful example of the fourth leader discipline: human capital developers. This leadership competency ensures that the leaders' organization has the skills required for future performance as well as for responding to current needs. Human capital developers enable the organization to develop a people plan that defines the skills and perspectives required for continuing achievement as the organization and its strategic goals evolve over time. In doing so, leaders also demonstrate creative, innovative, and unexpected solutions. For example, JP Morgan Chase has brought into the bank young PhD mathematicians and physicists, as well as finance experts, to provide analytic support to its equity and bond traders.

Over the last several years, we've collected data from thousands of managers through a 360-degree survey to assess leadership code competence. The pattern in our results is clear and illuminating: without doubt, the domain of human capital development has the lowest competence score for leaders across every industry and every region (table 7-1).

TABLE 7-1

Competence of business leaders in foundational disciplines

Leadership domain	Mean competence score*
Strategist	3.7
Executor	3.7
Talent manager	3.7
Human capital developer	3.5
Personal proficiency	3.8

Source: RBL survey.

*Mean self-evaluation score of over 20,000 managers participating in a 360-degree survey about their competence in various leadership domains. Participants were from diverse industries and various geographic regions globally. Score is on a scale of 1 to 5, where 1 = poor performance and 5 = outstanding performance.

The relevance of this to agile talent is obvious. The premise of agile talent is that as capability requirements change in response to technology or competitive changes or the performance expectations of investors and regulators, leaders must anticipate and respond to these needs. Leadership skill as a human capital developer is critical to this combination of insight and action. But as we will soon point out, all of the leadership disciplines contribute to success in utilizing agile talent for the benefit of the organization.

Personal Proficiency: Invest in Yourself

A fifth leadership discipline is personal proficiency. Effective leaders are good models. Strong leaders inspire loyalty and goodwill in others because they themselves act with integrity and trustworthiness. They provide a model of appropriate behavior to others—at all levels of the organization, as well as to agile talent operating on behalf of the organization—and deal with difficult situations in an open and evenhanded way. Other qualities they exemplify include clear thinking, self-insight, stress management, modeling lifelong learning, and taking care of oneself physically.

How Strong Leaders Make Agile Talent Work

What are the important leadership actions that lead to success in agile talent? As outlined earlier, executives described the top-five reasons for utilizing expert talent:

1. Increase availability of expertise

2. Reduce cost

3. Avoid adding permanent headcount

4. Increase the speed of getting things done

5. Externals challenge our thinking and assumptions

Executives have busy calendars and they face many issues and people competing for their time and attention. What are the high-value ways that leaders apply the leadership code to the effective use of agile talent? We focus on all of the five leadership dimensions.

Strategist: Providing the Sponsorship Needed

Effective strategists understand the impact of a few critical leader behaviors on the performance of external resources. In this regard, there is no more crucial area than ensuring the right level and kind of sponsorship.

In an earlier chapter, we reported an interesting finding from our survey of executives: slightly above half of responding leaders described their organization as effective in ensuring that the work of external resources was appropriately sponsored. This is good news for the satisfied half of the executives and worrisome for the remaining ones, who expressed concern or criticism. What does good sponsorship look like? We provide a number of key criteria in tool 7-1.

TOOL 7-1

How well do you sponsor agile talent?

Rate your organization on each criterion on a scale of 1 to 5, where 1 = almost never, and 5 = almost always. Then rate where you think other leaders in your organization stand on the same criteria.

Criterion for sponsoring agile talent	Self-rating	Rating of leaders in general
1. Demonstrates accountability and ownership for the business case and the decision to utilize external resources		
2. Ensures alignment with the organization's broader strategy and priorities		
3. Anticipates potential problems and risk factors		
4. Works closely with the team or individuals		
5. Ensures continuity of sponsorship over time		
6. Provides prompt feedback on successes and needs for improvement		
7. Supports the team or individuals		
8. Provides timely decisions		
9. Ensures sufficient resources		
10. Models ethical and honest working relationships		

After you have filled in tool 7-1, notice how the scores are distributed:

- Does the leadership of your organization provide a high-enough level of sponsorship for agile talent to deliver real value consistently?

- Are you satisfied with the quality of your sponsorship or that of your immediate boss?

If the answer to either or both questions is no, consider these additional questions:

- What are the critical areas for improvement?

- What is impeding excellence overall or in your specific case?

- Is your organization getting the value it needs from its investment in agile talent?

- What changes would you make to strengthen sponsorship?

Executor: Good Leaders Plan and Clear the Way

If a key deliverable of the strategist is providing the required sponsorship, the equivalent executor competency is the leader's role in clearing the way for the organization to achieve high performance. Steve Jobs was once asked who best exemplified what it takes for a business to be successful. He replied, "My model for business is the Beatles. They were four guys who kept each other's negative tendencies in check. They balanced each other, and the total was greater than the sum of the parts. That's how I see business: great things in business are never done by one person, they're done by a team of people."[2] Jobs's comment points out that putting the right people together with the right skills to achieve a clear and common goal is at the heart of execution. When agile talent is added to the mix, the way that leaders set goals, review performance, and build strong teams becomes even more important. The inclusion of agile talent in an organization raises an additional complexity: the need to build effective relationships between internal and external resources.

When the respondents in our survey were asked how well their organization brings together internal and external resources in common cause, we found an interesting mix. Slightly less than half of the executives in our study report that their organization does a good job of helping external resources build the right internal relationships to succeed. Another 30 percent are neutral, describing their organization as neither strong nor weak; 20 percent of executives are highly critical.

Google is a good example of an organization working hard to improve executor skills in its organization. Google's Project Oxygen, currently under way as a key research project in HR, focuses on what it takes to build and lead a great team. For example, Google has identified the importance of pairing challenging project goals with short time horizons.

IBM took a different tack in helping its software development managers be stronger team-building executors and focused on the career-stages research reviewed earlier. The company found that high-performing teams had more than the technical expertise required. The teams also had the right combination of career stages: namely, stage 1 and 2 individuals responsible for doing the work and stage 3 professionals and managers who managed work streams, coordinated the work of professionals, integrated their work with the efforts of other teams, and mentored and coached individuals. Stage 4 professionals, in turn, ensured that the teams had the resources and other support they needed and, when necessary, protected the team from interruption.

Another critical element in effective internal-external teamwork is simply time together. Katzenbach and Smith describe the importance of time for teamwork in his research on high-performing teams. A good example of making time is the Zappos quarterly "all-hands meeting," which combines information about company performance, team-building activities that include both internal and external talent, and inspirational guest speakers. Zappos also supports internal-external teamwork through its blog *Zappos Insights* as a way to keep people informed about performance and company events and activities. The blog is a powerful and simple way to engage external agile talent.

Ongoing performance feedback is another effective tool for effective internal-external teamwork. Our pilot study asked executives to describe how effective their organizations were in providing external resources with regular feedback on their contribution. We found a very similar trend to the findings for internal-external relationships: approximately 50 percent of executives report that their organizations provide externals with timely feedback on performance, 30 percent were neutral in their ratings, and 20 percent see a need for improvement.

Finally, executors are mindful of the need for ongoing improvement in the effectiveness of their organizations and what can be improved through tools like after-action review. As described earlier, after-action reviews are a US military tool created to improve learning from both successful projects and failures. We asked executives, "How well does the organization use after-action review to learn from the actions and results of external experts?" and found that only a third of executives were positive in their ratings of after-action review frequency and quality. An equal segment of executives was less sanguine, believing that their organization could use after-action review more often and effectively.

Talent Manager: Matchmaker for Development

The talent management aspect of good leadership plays an obviously critical role in agile talent. This manager ensures that the organization has the skills required to achieve today's goals, overcome performance challenges, and the systems in place to continue to sharpen employees' competencies and contribution.

Talent management starts with recognition of the skill set and competency mix required to achieve the team or organization's goals. Good leaders use a systematic approach to decide how to best resource an initiative. They understand the relative importance of a given task over other priorities and consider alternative resourcing approaches in light of short- and long-term benefits. They use a version of the strategic resourcing matrix to decide when it makes sense to own resources and when it makes more sense to rent or hire them, with the expectation that the agile talent is excited by a project opportunity but not interested in becoming a long-term employee. Mark Zuckerberg describes his philosophy of resourcing at Facebook as follows: "We want Facebook to be one of the best places people can go to learn how to build stuff. If you want to build a company, nothing is better than jumping in and trying to build one. But Facebook is also great for entrepreneurs/ hackers. If people want to come for a few years and move on and build something great, that's something we're proud of."[3]

A strong talent manager recognizes that selecting project leaders to work with or to oversee the external talent is an important decision. A recent study pointed out that among research labs in R&D organizations, the talent mix is the principal determinant of lab productivity.[4] When external experts are asked to describe great internal project managers with whom they have worked, they consistently report the following qualities listed in tool 7-2. You can use this tool to consider how well your organization applies the skills of talent manager to external resources and how well you do so yourself.

Using a matrix like the one in tool 7-3 helps leaders select project managers who will do a good job of managing externals and will grow professionally as a result of the experience. The optimal condition is the top left box: a dual emphasis on both performance and development. And this in turn requires that the organization have a process for assessing project management aptitude and performance and for supporting the development of project management competence.

Effective talent managers also build effective systems of development that link internal and external agile talent. Many organizations bring in expert externals, typically stage 3 or 4, to work as coaches for their younger leaders or for professionals that have run into performance difficulty. Norwegian multinational oil and gas company Statoil took this concept to the next level by creating "schools" in areas like

TOOL 7-2

How well does your organization manage agile talent?

Rate your organization on each criterion on a scale of 1 to 5, where 1 = almost never, and 5 = almost always. Then rate where you think other leaders in your organization stand on the same criteria.

Criterion for effectively managing agile talent	Self-rating	Rating of leaders in general
1. Well-defined, measurable individual and team goals		
2. Clear individual roles and role interdependencies ("Who depends on me?")		
3. Career stage consistent with the role and responsibilities		
4. Shared leadership philosophy and values		
5. Technical competence ensured, valued, and required		
6. Environment that promotes collaboration		
7. Effective problem-solving approach		
8. Performance culture: straight talk, feedback, culture of accountability and ownership for results		
9. Celebration of shared achievements		
10. Reasonable team turnover (people move on)		

oil-field project management, where leaders were explicitly connected to external experts in the area through educational opportunity and coaching. For Statoil, this was a critical initiative: despite the typically high level of Norwegian technical professionalism, the extreme, harsh climate of working in the North Sea and the Arctic Circle challenged Statoil to step up its effectiveness. A similar approach was used to build skills in other critical areas such as HR management. By combining coaching with education and work on key priorities, Statoil developed a unique cadre of talent in multiple areas.

Determining a prospective talent manager's emphasis in working with agile talent

Check which box in the matrix best represents the aptitude of the talent manager you are considering for developing and supporting your agile talent.

	High emphasis on development	Low emphasis on development
High emphasis on performance		
Low emphasis on performance		

Human Capital Developer: Build Ongoing Competence

Companies are utilizing agile talent because it offers them another route to the expertise they need to compete, perform, and grow. Partnerships with third-party agile talent continue to expand because organizations benefit from the access to expertise that enables them to increase strategic organizational capability and to deliver these capabilities more quickly, effectively, and cost-efficiently. We have described the implications of the strategist and executor roles of the leadership code, how organizations improve the use and performance of external experts. The role of human capital developer is particularly important because this aspect of good leadership prepares the organization for the future and is most likely to utilize agile, external talent.

The Leadership Code describes a number of skills that are at the heart of leadership competence in this area.[5] From the perspective of agile talent, effective leaders demonstrate excellence in human capital development when they think and act from the outside in.

The first test in outside-in thinking is what we call *mapping the workforce*. Mapping the workforce is another way of asking, Do we have the skills we will need to achieve our goals in the foreseeable future? In chapter 2, we described how organizations best assess the opportunity for agile talent. Uber, we mentioned, demonstrated this capability by recognizing that its strategy was linked longer term to self-driving cars and that robotics was going to be a critical area of technical expertise. Interestingly, Uber later ended up hiring the entire team, thus complicating efforts by other firms to make use of the Carnegie Mellon capability. By contrast, GoPro, the wearable-camera company, recently expanded its strategic vision to include other wearable technology. In this vein, it is working with a range of business and technical consultants in the fashion industry and with several joint ventures.

The agile-talent twist on mapping the workforce is that a good map includes both internal and external players. A leader who thinks of only internal resources and full-time employees has limited his or her resourcing options.

Mapping the workforce is the opener, but strong human capital developers also understand the importance of the organization's reputation as an employer of agile talent. Earlier, we discussed the importance of employer branding to the attraction and retention of external as well as internal agile talent. Talented external experts are typically in demand, have more opportunity than they can handle, and are disposed to work in organizations that value them and their contribution.

Our work with Driscoll's reinforces this point. As we mentioned, the leaders invested the necessary time in agile-talent orientation, ensuring that the external team understood and supported the company's vision and values.

As we said earlier, the leadership of Driscoll's recognized that our knowledge as leadership consultants and our commitment to its strategy and culture made a difference. By sharing the history and importance of the company vision and way of working, and by requiring that deliverables be framed in terms of the mission and values, the company made the external resources feel and act as partners rather than a pair of hands. Do we have evidence that this investment of time made a substantive difference? No. But by making their success our success, Driscoll's certainly raised the level of consultant ownership and pride.

Human capital developers take seriously their responsibility as skill and career developers and extend this responsibility to the agile talent with whom they work. For example, Google is broadly committed to publishing the results of innovative internal and external work as long as there is no strategy impairment. For external resources, this commitment is significant. Management and technical consultants often rely on the publicity surrounding their work as a means of gaining future project opportunities and building their reputation for expertise.

Human capital developers take an interest in the careers and development of external resources. Leaders have always been expected to mentor and coach internal employees, but cloud-resourcing logic invites leaders to also be open to doing the same thing for external talent as well. The very process of supporting a career through conversation and the demonstration of active interest builds engagement and improves the relationship.

Smart leaders also understand that today's consultant may be tomorrow's internal employee or leader. External agile talent has long considered the move from consultancy to client organization as an attractive career path. Leaders considering external experts have the benefit of seeing them in action. A thoughtful leader sees this talent as an important source of experienced recruits.

Outside-in thinking about emerging skills and needed capabilities encourages leaders to be active networkers. Smart leaders are eager to learn how other organizations are approaching opportunity or responding to similar challenges. External resources are an excellent source of industry insight and innovation. For example, we were recently asked by the chief HR officer of Hewlett-Packard to give her team a presentation on strategic talent issues facing high-technology companies. Similarly, Bill Allen, head of HR at Macy's, made it a point to engage us in a series of discussions about the future of HR with his top managers before initiating an HR organizational transformation. And Pat Hedley, a managing director of the private equity giant General Atlantic, agreed to chair a newly formed private-equity HR association to stay up-to-date on HR trends in her industry.

More fundamentally, leaders who operate from the outside-in tend to build inclusive rather than exclusive cultures. We talked earlier about the importance of engaging external resources from day one and the value of treating this important element of your overall workforce with respect and trust rather than suspicion. A leader who encourages networks and a broad set of external relationships is more likely to appreciate what it takes for agile talent to learn how to perform in a new organizational environment. And the leader is more likely to provide a sufficient orientation and introductions to facilitate the individual's success. In a savvy leader's view, the individual is a part of the organization's larger performance system rather than a temporary intruder.

Effective human capital developers also invest in giving their employees outside experiences, so that the workers are sensitive to other cultures and organizational environments and are more likely to welcome and cooperate with external resources. The great global consumer products company P&G invests significantly in training and development because leaders over multiple generations of management have found that employees who have these outside experiences are more collaborative, team oriented, and open to other points of view.

We think a similar result occurs when companies invest time in building relationships between internal and external experts. In the Gallup survey of engagement, the most committed people have work relationships that matter to them.[6] Organizations can take advantage of this association between meaningful work and engagement by offering its workers appropriate assignments and by building communities of practice that support diversity or technical skills. These communities operate most effectively when they are inclusive, not divisive. Leaders need to ensure that external talent is both welcomed into these communities and expected to contribute best practices and innovative ways of working as a condition of employment. Strong networks lead to faster learning and more collaboration.

Personal Proficiency Ties It All Together

Unlike the preceding leadership competencies, personal proficiency is about the model a leader presents through his or her actions, choices, way of solving problems, and values. We've always enjoyed the question, very fitting in the context of personal proficiency, "Why would anyone want to be led by you?" This question has special meaning for agile talent.

A personally proficient leader expresses his or her humanity in dealings with agile talent. These leaders understand that beyond the technical or functional requirements of the work itself, the most difficult aspects of agile-talent work are often personal and interpersonal. Operating as a consultant, an external adviser, a freelance software architect, or any other external expert can be a lonely existence. And it is often a challenging one: a person faces the loneliness of working in a new organization, the stresses of coming and going on assignment from workplace to workplace, getting to know and work with new people and their individuality, and learning to operate effectively in new organizational environments, each with their own unique culture.

When all is said and done, effective leadership is an act of generosity. Good leaders are remembered as being generous with their time, hospitable to colleagues and guests, and willing mentors. All of these qualities are as important to external talent as they are to internal talent. The leadership qualities described by the personal proficiency competency create high-performance environments for part-time and temporary as well as permanent staff.

Summary

This chapter reviewed how the actions and skills of leaders have a significant impact on the effectiveness of agile talent. Leaders who have the competencies of the leadership code are more able to build high-performance organizations and create an environment of inclusion that attracts and retains agile talent—whether the talent is there for a gig, a project, or a career.

In the last several chapters, we've described the alignment challenge in getting the most from agile talent. The results of our survey suggest that the skills required by leaders who wish to make the most of agile-talent resourcing are often well in place. This is good news. Many of the executives report positively on their organization's efforts to set appropriate goals, anticipate potential problems and difficulties, establish relationships between internal staff and external talent, and provide helpful feedback and communication updates. We also found that consistently between 25 and 35 percent of executives are less fulsome in their assessments, are more critical of their organization's handling of external resources, and asserted that their organizations had both the opportunity and the need to improve.

In the next chapter, we turn from aligning the organization to leading the change, the next step in securing agile talent.

8

Leading the Change

Driving Innovation in How Your
Organization Manages Talent

We know the challenges of agile talent are on the rise.[1] According to Plunkett Research, global revenues for established consultancies (combining HR, IT, strategy, operations, and business advisory services) totaled $431 billion in 2014, up 4 percent from 2013.[2] That agile talent is a global phenomenon is shown in the fact that the US share of these revenues is $180 billion, less than half the global total. The data only includes revenue figures reported by consulting firms with more than one person. Plunkett mentions the one-person businesses in the summary to its 2014 research report: "In contrast to the size and infrastructure of the leading management consulting companies, a large portion of the industry is comprised of very small companies—in many cases these are one-person shops, perhaps operating from a spare bedroom at home. This part of the business has grown rapidly."[3]

Whether agile talent is a firm or an individual, the challenge of change is always significant, and particularly so for cloud resourcing. In this chapter, we focus on a framework to guide agile-talent planning, we identify key threats to successful change, and we offer readers several tools and techniques that provide practical guidance during change management.

Variations on Agile Talent

In a global economy embracing agile talent, it makes sense that organizations are taking different paths in gaining the advantage of what it offers. As described earlier, there are three alternative paths a company can take.

The Traditional Path

The traditional path is the null version of agile talent, and it is probably the situation in which most organizations find themselves. In this approach, leaders of traditionally structured and managed organizations choose to take greater advantage of what these new opportunities offer on an exception basis. The traditional version of agile talent requires the least change; the dominant logic of strategy and organization is that a significant majority of work will continue to be performed by full-time, permanent employees and that external experts will primarily be drawn into work on an exception basis, where their skills are strategically important and generally available. "Rent the best, and ensure success" is the mantra of this approach. We believe that for the foreseeable future, the traditional approach is likely to continue to be the most prevalent version of agile talent.

The Transformational Path

Organizations that depend on virtual organization structures are uncommon, but there are a few. Industries such as motion pictures and other entertainment offer a glimpse of the possibilities of working with the agile talent of the future. For example, many of today's movies are funded by a myriad of production companies. And in the movie credits, it's not unusual to see scores of supporting firms that have provided services from health and safety for the cast and crew to leased lighting equipment.

Software start-ups in Silicon Valley are the leading industry that is comfortable with the transformational approach. Andreesen Horowitz, a well-known investment firm, trumpets its competitive edge as the ability to connect start-up companies to the company's unique agile-talent network. And described earlier, a growing number of agile-talent organizations operate on a community model where independent experts come together from across independent firms to work on joint projects, and the firm provides basic administrative services. Cordence, now a community of over two thousand consultants, enjoys aggregate revenues of over $600 million. Interestingly, Cordence consultants are generally happier with their organization than are most consultants.[4]

The Surgical Capability Growth Path

This third category, surgical capability growth, describes organizations that choose to take a more selective, or surgical approach, to the use of agile talent. In this case, agile talent is applied to accelerate capability development or change. The surgical path is an intermediate state between traditional and transformational approaches to agile talent. For example, as Michael Lewis observes in his book *Flash Boys*, as high-speed trading became a critical capability for brokerage firms, the industry could not find sufficient full-time talent.[5] There were few technical experts who had the competence to create the new equity trading platforms and private exchanges that were required to meet the expansion of the business. To remain competitive in this new world, firms relied on agile talent and other resourcing arrangements to quickly grow their capability. For example, the Disney Institute grew over time, but early in its history, it brought in a core group of agile talent, including consultants and executive education specialists, to power its early growth and development.

———————

Table 8-1 presents some advantages and disadvantages of the three approaches to agile talent and gives some examples of companies using each one. Despite the distinctions in these approaches, we also know that they intersect. In the movie industry, a transformational catalyst, the breakup of the so-called Hollywood studio system in the early 1950s and the introduction of independent production companies, shifted the use of agile talent from traditional to transformational. As the producer role gained in influence, producers developed their own virtual teams, which they regularly brought together to plan, make, and distribute their movies. Relationships between the producers and their favorite directors, cast, and crew created the modern movie production: an intense, high-performing cast with some individuals involved for years and others for only months or weeks.

The path to transformational change in agile talent is incremental; organizations shift from a traditional resourcing format to the intermediate state we've described as surgical capability growth. Few organizations outside of industries like finance and entertainment have gone all the way to transformation, and we believe that most organizations may, in fact, continue to operate fundamentally in a traditional manner. But

TABLE 8-1

The three approaches to agile talent

	Traditional	Transformational	Surgical
Example	JP Morgan Chase	Sony Pictures	Walt Disney Institute
Resourcing strategy	The organization primarily relies on full-time, permanent employees.	Most company associates are independent agents brought together on a project basis.	Company selectively uses external experts to build strategic capability.
Resource base	Most associates continue to be in a traditional employment relationship.	There is a small full-time employee base, mostly in administrative or central functions such as finance.	Most associates remain full-time employees; a higher percentage of external experts are in the new capability area.
Change readiness	Readiness is typically lower, but it depends on the organization.	Readiness is high; the organization can change quickly and dynamically.	Readiness is high; the organization can bring on new external resources quickly.
Managerial challenge	Managers face traditional challenges.	Managers must juggle multiple independent priorities.	Managers must identify the expertise required for superior capability.
Reward challenge for top performers	For internal staff, the reward is above-average pay and rapid promotional opportunity.	For external experts, the reward should be negotiated with top external experts; it could include bonus or back-end participation, or equity.	The reward is a combination of traditional and transformational. There may be different incentives for external experts than for full-time staff operating in the same unit.
Potential pitfall	The organization might fail to put in place alignments that increase agile-talent productivity.	The organization might build a large internal staff that competes with the free-agency project model.	The organization might make bad strategic choices about the organizational capabilities required for success.
Growth edge	Make greater use of agile talent as appropriate.	Be innovative about where you can use external experts and how they can increase your organization's effectiveness and efficiency, e.g., simulation, rehearsal.	The growth edge is similar to that of the transformational approach: be innovative about where you can use external experts and how they can increase your organization's effectiveness and efficiency.

clearly, global experience in business process outsourcing, together with increased availability of agile talent in developing countries, has led organizational leaders to feel more confident and potentially more adventurous about broadening and deepening their use of external resourcing.

The Challenge of Change

Determining the depth and focus of involvement in agile talent is a critical first step for any leader. Whether the organization is incrementally upping its involvement in agile talent, tapping the cloud for help quickly and powerfully building specific capability, or aiming over time to fundamentally transform the way the organization chooses to resource work, there is the practical challenge of managing change. In prior chapters, we have described some of the specific areas where change is required or beneficial. In this chapter, we provide a more integrative view of how an organization should approach the change process. And we show how cultural issues that arise in the course of change are best identified and addressed. Without question, leaders skilled at managing change—strategically and culturally—are more likely to achieve their goals.[6]

The Mind-Set of Successful Change

Imagine some great television interviewer in conversation with a trio of corporate chief executives, all of whom are reflecting on the shift in their organization's resourcing philosophy. Although each of the three companies is in a different industry—banking, pharmaceuticals, and supply-chain logistics—and while each CEO is from a different continent, the companies clearly have some experiences in common.

Change Is Essential

This is the first point on which the CEOs agree. Change is essential as an ongoing response to shifting external and internal trends and circumstances. The leader's role is to make sure the company is adapting—changing—in the best possible way. With respect to each company's relationship to agile talent specifically, one of the most important messages a leader can send is the necessity of a more complex internal and external approach to staffing. We earlier pointed out that the leadership code factor where most managers are weakest is human capital developer, which requires understanding and meeting the talent needs of the organization in the future. In this context, it is crucial that leaders help their people understand why the organization is likely to depend more significantly on external resourcing, how a richer mix of resources will affect how the organization works, and what the shifts mean for full-time employees.

Change Is Hard

Change is resisted because it is hard. That's the second conclusion of the CEOs in our pilot study. And change is hard because it is complex. We all know the statistic that 70 percent of change efforts do not achieve their goals; that observation, popularized by John Kotter, has been reported broadly.[7] A second statistic makes this lack of successful change even more interesting and meaningful: 90 percent of change efforts began with a technically sound problem diagnosis and implementation plan.[8] For many full-time employees, the increased use of agile talent implies greater hassle in dealing with people who are not "us" and whose loyalty and motivation are suspect. Full-time employees may fear that working with externals also means risk: risk of losing a job, changing a career, or moving to a new city.

We have seen this us-versus-them mentality play out in divisive ways in many organizations working with agile talent. The expert model in consulting exacerbates the problem and is difficult to change because most of the large firms are dependent on this business model. In the expert model, a large team of experts enters into your organization to solve a problem using their superior industry knowledge. The process of outside experts solving problems and then handing off the solution for implementation to internals creates resistance. To address this issue, we have utilized a more collaborative approach that is an alternative to the expert model. We call this approach the *capability transfer model*. Rather than sending in a large team of experts to solve the problem, we utilize a smaller team of more senior external experts who work with a combination of teams that are set up internally with the client to work with our agile talent. In the kind of work we do, these internal teams typically consist of a *working team*, seven to ten internal, high-potential influencers who go through a guided process with our senior external experts to create a roadmap for change. The roadmap includes a diagnostic and a plan for implementation. This team meets periodically with a second team of senior sponsor-level executives who provide guidance and support and who ultimately make decisions based on the recommendations of the working group and external talent. This process enables an everyone-is-us attitude rather than an us-versus-them climate. The process also accelerates change because the internals now really own the change.

Change Is Personal

Change is also hard because it's personal. And for the architects of change, the decision makers, it's often not personal. It's what happens to people at lower levels of the organization. Take the case of

Undercover Boss, an internationally franchised reality television show that places well-disguised company CEOs or other top leaders of organizations on the front lines of their own organization. The premise of the show works because we want executives to experience what the rest of us experience each day. And that is the challenge for leaders, to understand how the changes they are making will affect the work and motivation of the people who must implement the change. In every episode of *Undercover Boss*, the CEO of the company has some kind of epiphany about how ideas translated into action have an impact on people's lives personally.

The capability transfer model of change also addresses the personal nature of change. In the expert model, a sophisticated resolution of the problem is handed off to internals for implementation. People resist change that they don't own. They don't own the expert model, because they have not been part of the change. They often believe that significant internal issues (politics, culture, and so on) have been missed or ignored by the outside experts, who focus primarily on a content resolution to whatever the challenge is. In the capability transfer model, the internal issues have been vetted by the internal working team and again by the sponsor teams. The process itself drives buy-in to change from the beginning.

Change Occurs at Multiple Levels

Finally, change follows its own path, despite our efforts to precisely engineer it. A timeless quote from the movie *Jurassic Park* illustrates this point: "If there's one thing the history of evolution has taught us, it's that life will not be contained. Life breaks free. It expands to new territories. It crashes through barriers painfully, maybe even dangerously, but—well, there it is."[9]

Change is similar. And while it cannot be fully controlled, its unin-
tended consequences can be anticipated. We think of four directions
of change: what are the likely impacts on individuals, the team, the
organization, and external stakeholders such as customers? Agile talent is likely to affect all of these levels, and a smart leadership team
carefully considers both the probable and possible results of this
change and takes proactive steps where possible.

The Pilot's Checklist

A recent study of technology developments by Jim Johnson and colleagues found that initiatives were more likely to be successful when
five factors were present:[10]

- **EXECUTIVE SUPPORT**: According to Johnson and his colleagues,
  the lack of executive support, or the wrong sponsorship, is the
  number one factor in project failure.

- **USER INVOLVEMENT**: A project will fail if it doesn't meet the
  needs or expectations of its users or customers, and is more
  likely to fail when the users are not actively involved.

- **EXPERIENCED PROJECT MANAGEMENT**: Successful projects
  invariably have an experienced and talented project manager
  leading the work.

- **CLEAR BUSINESS OBJECTIVES**: Project success follows from
  setting the right objectives and ensuring that these objectives
  are clear, kept up front, and revisited frequently.

- **MINIMIZED SCOPE CHANGE**: Scope changes are as fraught in IT
  projects as in building construction. Effective project managers
  plan up front and keep scope changes to a minimum.

While Johnson and his colleague's research is specific to IT project management, the findings are similar in concept to the *pilot's checklist*, a change-management framework originally developed by Dave Ulrich, Steve Kerr, and others to support the GE Work-Out program. The pilot's checklist is a tool that we have used in virtually every project we have undertaken at the RBL Group. The pilot's checklist honors the tradition of an airplane pilot walking around the airplane, inspecting the aircraft's flight-worthiness, before takeoff. The value of the checklist is that it ensures a sharp focus on the factors that will make or break the success of the pilot's mission. So too with the change version of pilot's checklist.

The pilot's checklist identifies seven basic requirements for successful change management. The framework was initially created as a checklist to aid work teams addressing specific improvement projects to make sure that projects came in on time and on budget.

Tool 8-1 is a pilot's checklist of requirements for a successful change venture. Read the requirements, keeping in mind a recent change effort at your organization. Then rate each requirement to identify what led to the success or failure of the change venture.

Involve the External Expert Community

Applying the pilot's checklist is helpful in identifying what may get in the way of a viable plan to make greater use of agile talent. A not-very-well-used but potentially helpful source of information is the external experts who know your organization best. This agile talent may be able to provide unique insight on how the organization is unintentionally harming its efforts to drive greater cloud resourcing; for example, excessive payment delays may lead key agile talent to choose to work for a competitor. Table 8-2 suggests some potential impediments to success.

TOOL 8-1

The pilot's checklist: identifying what leads to the success or failure of a change venture

---

Rate your organization on a scale from 1 to 5, where 1 = disagree strongly, and 5 = agree strongly.

Requirement	Rating
Executive sponsorship: We have clear and sufficient executive sponsorship and support.	
Shared belief in the need for change: There is sufficient broad agreement about the importance of the actions we are taking and why these actions are important and necessary to the organization.	
Clear and compelling goals: The goals are sufficiently clear and compelling to the individuals who are involved.	
Supportive stakeholders: The stakeholders for this change effort— individuals who must support or at least be non-antagonistic to the actions taken—are sufficiently supportive.	
Well-defined game plan and decision gates: The plan for this change effort is sufficiently detailed and defined, and the critical decisions are well enough identified.	
Sufficient human, technical, and financial resources: The critical and essential resources are in place or available as needed.	
Learning, adapting, and monitoring: A process is sufficiently in place for key actors and team members to review and assess progress, identify problems, and address impending issues.	

Dealing with Cultural Obstacles to Change

The pilot's checklist offers a roadmap for effective change management, but it doesn't explicitly address cultural obstacles to the change that leaders intend to put in place. All organizations have cultural elements that resist change; while some companies are more suspicious of external experts and resist using them, PepsiCo and Mars regularly work with a wide range of consultancies.

TABLE 8-2

How externals might rate the pilot's checklist

Requirement	Potential impediments that agile talent might identify
Executive sponsorship	• Conflicting executive opinions about the problem or the solution • Competing leadership views about the priority of the work; agreement needed on the priorities or readiness to take action • Indications of covert political agendas that will impede third-party performance; lack of required transparency for the work to be successful
Shared belief in the need for change	• Lack of employee confidence that the organization will take the required action; declining conviction from the people who must own and implement the work • Lack of agreement that the organization is in a position to take action
Clear and compelling goals	• Failure to think in terms of discrete performance units and specific, measurable goals • Lack of clarity about who is responsible for what decisions • Scope creep, which will impede performance and must be avoided
Supportive stakeholders	• Views of key stakeholders not incorporated or poorly incorporated into the planning and execution of the work • Different stakeholder groups not well managed
Well-defined game plan and decision gates	• Lack of detailed roadmap • Failure to determine key performance gates or phases—where an explicit decision is required • Poorly defined critical decision points • Failure to clarify which measures will be used to decide • Lack of clarity about who is involved in each decision gate
Sufficient human, technical, and financial resources	• Failure to identify resources required at each phase of the work • Inadequately resourcing the work • Failure to address the process and timing of resource availability and placement in response to a change of scope
Learning, adapting, and monitoring	• Inadequate monitoring of progress • No organizational learning agenda for this work, separate from performing the work • Poor communication of work progress and performance to stakeholders

Using the organization virus detector: identifying the three most important cultural risk factors in managing change in your organization

The RBL Group uses this cultural virus tool to help teams of managers identify organization risk factors and then share how they manifest and what could be done to eliminate them. The full tool has thirty-six common viruses that impede change. Managers are asked to select one or two viruses that they consider the most threatening to the organization's ability to work effectively. The complete virus detector can be licensed from the RBL Group.

Common cultural risk factors, or viruses, in managing change in your organization (sample viruses)

1. *Overinform:* We meet and meet again before we decide, which slows down decisions.
2. *Have it my way:* We don't learn from each other; "not invented here" syndrome.
3. *Good, but . . . :* Criticism is a company sport. We always find something wrong.
4. *False positive:* We agree in person, then disagree in private.
5. *We know best:* We know what our customers need far better than they do.

Some years ago, we created a tool to help leaders explicate the cultural barriers to change in their organizations. We called it the *organization virus detector*. For example, the HR leadership of TASC, a large high-tech contractor to the Pentagon, identified cultural factors as far more of a risk factor than financial or technical issues. As chief HR officer Jim Lawler put it at one of our meetings, "We have outstanding technical skill and strong financial backing. But, to grow, we need to develop a more agile culture."

Test your organization's cultural challenges to change. Bring a small group of your organization's managers together to review and discuss an upcoming opportunity to involve external experts in an important project or initiative. Ask each manager to identify what he or she sees as three of the critical cultural obstacles to the success of this venture. Then bring the right group of people together to resolve the issue. For example, one manager might identify "activity mania—we like to be so busy that we don't set or manage priorities."

Once each leader has chosen his or her three potential obstacles, share the lists and agree on the three that are most worrisome for this particular undertaking.

Finally, as a leadership team, discuss what can and must be done to reduce and hopefully eliminate the negative impact of the viruses. Tool 8-2 lists many of the most common viruses that impede change. You can use this tool to help you identify your most worrisome obstacles.

The Road to Abilene

A favorite teaching moment of ours was created years ago by Professor Jerry Harvey.[11] Harvey described what he called the Abilene paradox; alternatively, it has come to be known as the paradox of agreement. The fable goes as follows:

> On a hot afternoon visiting in Coleman, Texas, the family is comfortably playing dominoes on a porch, until the father-in-law suggests that they take a trip to Abilene [fifty-three miles north] for dinner. The wife says, "Sounds like a great idea." The husband, despite having reservations because the drive is long and hot, thinks that his preferences must be out-of-step with the group and says, "Sounds good to me. I just hope your mother wants to go." The mother-in-law then says, "Of course I want to go. I haven't been to Abilene in a long time."

The drive *is* hot, dusty, and long. When they arrive at the cafeteria, the food is as bad as the drive. They arrive back home four hours later, exhausted.

One of them dishonestly says, "It was a great trip, wasn't it?" The mother-in-law says that, actually, she would rather have stayed home, but went along since the other three were so enthusiastic. The husband says, "I wasn't delighted to be doing what we were doing. I only went to satisfy the rest of you." The wife says, "I just went along to keep you happy. I would have had to be crazy to want to go out in the heat like that." The father-in-law then says that he only suggested it because he thought the others might be bored.

The group sits back, perplexed that they together decided to take a trip which none of them wanted. They each would have preferred to sit comfortably, but did not admit to it when they still had time to enjoy the afternoon.[12]

The message of the Abilene fable is to manage the journey actively, and this suggests an additional tool of change management we might call *second session C*. The original session C is an invention of General Electric. Twice annually, the executive team, starting with CEO Jeff Immelt, reviews the organization and talent of each of GE's businesses. We suggest the addition of a semiannual corporate review of agile-talent activity within the organization. Leaders ought to regularly and systematically ask how well the organization is utilizing its agile talent; discussion should include problematic areas and ways in which the organization is performing brilliantly in how it seeks and works with external help. We expand on this approach in the next chapter.

Summary

As organizations develop an increasing depth and range of agile-talent solutions, change management becomes a more critical skill. As other chapters have pointed out, the culture and human capital practices of the organization will have a significant impact on the reaction to third-party experts and on the effectiveness of their productivity. However, leaders have ways to better manage the change processes and the behavior of the organization to increase the effectiveness of its agile talent. In the next and last chapter of the book, we take a broader lens and consider how agile talent is developing and its implications for the future.

9

Turning What We Know into What We Do

Making Agile Talent Work

Saul Alinsky, the great Chicago social activist and community organizer, wrote his iconic book *Rules for Radicals* as "a practical primer for realistic radicals."[1] We wish we had written that sentence. It describes perfectly the intent of our book. In our view, agile talent is the point of the spear leading to a profound change in the way organizations structure and resource their activities. The agile-talent approach has far-reaching implications for workforce planning, the way that work teams are constructed, and the way that future generations of experts think about and manage their careers. And agile talent significantly influences how leaders manage and lead change.

In this final chapter we turn to the key opportunities and challenges that agile talent offers a forward-thinking organization. Then, we propose key steps in the ninety-day plan (described below) for preparing your organization to make the best possible use of agile talent.

Agile Talent Will Continue to Be More of a Factor in Strategy

As strategy researchers Rita McGrath and David Teece point out, agile talent represents a powerful means for companies to *rapidly* increase their technical and functional competence. Companies locate this competence where it needs to be located to build the strategic capabilities the organization requires to meet the competitive challenge of new, disruptive entrants.

Phillip Morris International offers a useful example. The shift away from paper cigarettes to electronic devices that reduce tar and nicotine—the shift being a profound change driven by health concerns and global regulation—led senior management to kick off a transformation of the organization. When Charles Bendotti, HR executive for Phillip Morris Asia moved to Hong Kong in 2012, he quickly recognized the need for change in the size, structure, and capability of the HR organization. Assembling the right team was his first task, and the team he assembled combined high-potential HR staff from company headquarters and from across the region. He brought in top HR talent from Australia, South Africa, India, and Korea. But Bendotti also attracted a team of experienced HR and change professionals from leading consulting and advisory organizations such as the RBL Group, Accenture, and Korn Ferry to guide the change initiative and to provide the "gray hair" experience that the short deadline for change required. Once the changes were designed and implemented over an eighteen-month period, the external talent exited.

Agile Talent Is a Work in Progress

We know from the executives participating in our agile-talent study that effective management of agile talent is a work in progress. Overall, 20 to 25 percent of the executives completing the survey were fairly critical of their organization's capability and readiness to utilize agile talent. On some topics, a much larger percentage responded with concerns, for example, in describing how well external resources were oriented and onboarded, how well organizations anticipated potential problems, and the importance of keeping external resources informed and up-to-date on key issues likely to affect their work. Improvements in these areas would have a marked impact on the external experts' performance and their satisfaction.

Although a 70 percent failure rate in leading change is cause for concern, there is also reason for optimism. About half the executives in our study were generally positive about how effectively their organization selected and used agile talent. These executives pointed out that their organizations were doing an OK or a better job of ensuring that externally resourced work had the right level of sponsorship, that they built effective relationships between internal and external resources, and that administrative procedures treated external resources more as partners than as transactional vendors.

Agile Talent Invites Us to Rethink How We Organize

The management author Charles Handy anticipated agile talent in forecasting how organizations are likely to resource their activities in future. He called his model the "shamrock organization," and writing

FIGURE 9-1

Handy's prescient model of the shamrock organization: predicting the role of external agile talent

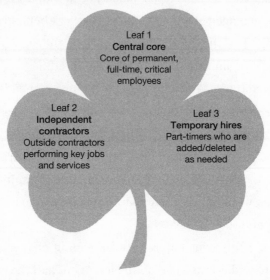

Source: Charles Handy, *The Age of Unreason* (Boston: Harvard Business School Press, 1990).

over twenty years ago, Handy presciently posited a futuristic organization model resembling the three leaves of a shamrock (figure 9-1).[2]

As Handy describes it, the first leaf consists of professionals and managers whose skills define the organization's core competence (we would say strategic capabilities). This core group defines what the company does and what business it is in. The next two leaves focus on agile talent as a means of supplementing internal staff through ongoing relationships with contractors providing strategic assistance and temporary workers who supplement the administrative and operational capacity of the organization.

Agile talent facilitates the shamrock by enabling organizations in two key areas: capability and flexibility. Through agile talent, the organization can supplement internal expertise, providing quick-turnaround access to skills that are not available within the organization or are unavailable because internals are preoccupied with other important work. Participants in our executive survey told us that external expertise also increases the speed of getting things done and the ability to staff up more expeditiously in response to opportunities or threats. Moreover, agile talent offers the organization the benefit of learning from the expertise of external specialists and the implications of their work with other clients or from other industries. This outside knowledge helps the organization test and challenge its own plans and assumptions.

Agile talent also makes it possible to "bolt on" new capabilities. We think of this as Lego organization design. A good example is provided by the case of Capital One, the financial services organization. Capital One is a leader in using social media and other technologies to improve the customer experience and increase "stickiness," or loyalty. This focus recently led the company to acquire Adaptive Path, a San Francisco–based customer experience consultancy. The entire firm moved over to Capital One as a captive expert operating independently within Capital One. As Adaptive Path cofounder and chief creative officer Jesse Garrett put it, "Somebody came along who finally, truly, seemed to get it. A company with a great culture that shares and values our intellectual curiosity and design sensibilities, that wants us to continue doing great work inside their organization, but also continue helping others do great work too, by fostering dialogue and teaching what we have learned. And that somebody, remarkably, turned out to be Capital One."[3] Interestingly, Adaptive Path continues to face the external market and curates a range of public workshops and events, further benefiting both the reputation and the insight of Capital One.

George Lucas's creative juggernaut, Industrial Light and Magic (ILM), the company that created *Star Wars* and *Indiana Jones*, is another example of the impact of agile talent on structure and resourcing, equipping organizations with greater ability to expand and contract as needed to respond to new opportunity. *Businessweek* describes the company's approach to resourcing this way:

> ILM has a permanent staff of about 700, but that can swell by as much as a quarter in the winter and spring, when effects work is being done on the summer blockbusters. Around 350 people at the Presidio worked with Farrar on *Transformers*, more than were actually on set with director Michael Bay. And John Knoll, visual effects supervisor on the third *Pirates of the Caribbean*, figures half of his team members were new to ILM. It's a significant challenge to accommodate the constantly rising and falling army of freelancers, all of whom need IT training and HR orientation, a computer (or three), and a place to sit. [4]

We like this quote for the clarity of ILM's resourcing strategy: ramping up and scaling down through agile talent is how ILM does business and influences everything, from how it organizes to how it sets up facilities. And what it says to ILM staff is crucial: importing external talent is not about replacing employees with cheaper, contingent, external staff. Agile talent is part of the ongoing talent equation at ILM. Lucas and the ILM leadership team think about the company's workforce holistically and inclusively, and agile talent is how the company ramps up or scales down according to its needs. There is no hard-edged boundary that defines "us" versus "them."

The acceptance of agile talent as a savvy and strategic business decision is a critical point. A few years ago, research by Ron Ash and Venkat Bendapudi at University of Kansas looked carefully at how permanent employees reacted to the use of consultants and other external resources. They found that context was key. When the externals primarily provided a means of reducing cost, there was far greater internal staff resistance than when the role of external expertise was to increase organizational performance through product or service innovation. A useful recent example of how *not* to use agile talent is offered by Disney. At the end of 2014, Disney decided to let 250 IT professionals go from its Orlando park organization and transferred the work to Indian technical professionals brought over under temporary visas. And in many cases, the soon-to-be-laid-off individuals were required to train their replacements. The decision created a PR problem for Disney and has hurt its reputation within the broader employment community of Central Florida. As one former employee reported to the *New York Times*, "I couldn't believe that they could fly people in to sit at our desks and take over our jobs."[5]

Agile Talent Relies on Strong Internal-External Partnerships

Shelley Seifert, the chief administrative officer of First Bank, a top US regional bank, was reflecting on the best-in-class improvement initiative she led at National City Corporation. Between 2005 and 2007, National City's best-in-class initiative captured almost $700 million in cost savings and increased revenues with the help of consultants and teams of internal experts. She describes her experience this way:

> A big lesson for us was the need to create a real partnership with the firms we'd brought in to help us. That meant we would need to show up with as strong a team as we expected from our external partners, which wasn't possible without executive team and functional managers' commitment. It's all uphill until everybody on the team embraces the same objective. Another significant lesson is that you want your external partners to give you their best ideas. That means accepting criticism, and sometimes it's

harsh criticism. But if you want to change, you must be open to the critique. Finally, and particularly important, you must think of the organization and the external resources as equal players— it's hard to do that when you think of yourselves as the client, but otherwise, you won't get the best work from your partners, who were hired by your company because they bring a valuable perspective. You won't get the full value if you aren't open and listening to their ideas, particularly the more challenging ones.[6]

Seifert's message is a powerful one. And it is consistently repeated by ILM, Capital One, and other organizations that are innovating in how they use and partner with external resources.

How do organizations create stronger and more enduring partnerships between internal staff and external resources? Innovative organizations have made this happen a number of ways:

- **UP-FRONT INVESTMENT IN THE RELATIONSHIP:** Among the ways that organizations establish strong internal-external resource partnerships, an effective orientation is both powerful and often overlooked. Orientation increases the engagement of external agile talent by providing critical context orientation. It reinforces internal-external teamwork when the team members, working with external resources, participate in onboarding and orientation activity. For example, several years ago Imperial Oil, the Canadian subsidiary of Exxon Mobil, hired a consulting team from Towers Watson to conduct an internal organization review after a major acquisition. Before kicking off the project, Imperial senior management sent a small team of senior line and HR staff to spend the day with the consulting team and familiarize themselves with the organization and its history, culture, and operating style. The visit made a powerful impression on the Towers Watson consultants. Imperial's open, engaged attitude showed its commitment to the initiative and to the partnership Imperial intended to create with its consultants. Not surprisingly, the initiative was a significant success.

- **USE OF PHYSICAL SPACE TO BUILD TEAMWORK**: When Duke Energy hired our firm to design a new strategy and organization for its HR function, the first action by the work's sponsor, Marc Manley, was to carve out a "homeroom" for the consulting team and the internal staff that would be partnering on the work. The homeroom was a place where internal and external team members could work together and informally bat around ideas to help the HR function achieve its cost and service goals. There was nothing fancy about the space; in fact, it was less a conference area and more a closet. But the impact on teamwork was considerable.

- **GIVE-AND-TAKE SESSIONS**: When National City brought Bain Capital in to assist a best-in-class initiative, a seemingly simple activity made a big difference in the quality of the work. Informal give-and-take sessions brought together the external agile talent and internal staff in a casual environment to share what they were learning and discuss what actions the organization should take to improve profitability. These sessions were frequent, usually in the evening, and often went quite late. But because of these give-and-takes, a strong bond formed among team members and significantly contributed to the success of the work.

- **REGULAR FEEDBACK**: Similar to the give-and-take sessions just described, AXA Equitable, an insurance company, undertook a process of "work out" to reinforce a 10 percent reduction in headcount by eliminating low-value work. Over the six months of the project, AXA started to hold regular feedback meetings between the external talent leading the work and the HR leadership team sponsoring the effort. The meetings turned out to be a very helpful move. The HR staff was engaged and informed, was able to respond to line-executive queries far better, and had the knowledge to support the activity and intervene as needed to keep it on track. And the external experts conducting the work had a very valuable feedback channel that helped them understand the impact of their work and see where changes were needed.

- **AFTER-ACTION REVIEW:** After-action review is a powerful problem-solving and change-management methodology that invites the principals of a project or an initiative to review what happened, why it happened, and what lessons learned from the experience could be helpful in future projects. TASC (now Engility), a major government contractor, used after-action reviews very productively in evaluating the workforce strategy it had implemented. Through such review, the company could address how it needed to change, given the new requirements of government purchasing policy and TASC's own future acquisition plans. Doing so gave TASC senior management a very clear view of the limitations of its workforce strategy process and how it needed to be redesigned.

Agile Talent Encourages Us to Rethink Talent Management

Agile talent doesn't ask us to throw away how we practice talent management. There is no expectation that we will recruit fundamentally differently, that traditional models of talent management will be sent to the dust pile, that we'll end investments in training and development, or that we'll do away with managerial roles (although Zappos is attempting to do just that). But beyond these fundamentals, expect that the agile-talent approach will change how we think about and act on talent issues. It does so by proposing that we apply many of the same principles of internal talent management to the way we deal with, and invest in, external talent.

As quoted earlier, Mark Zuckerberg threw the first punch in his description of professional development at Facebook: "Facebook is also great for entrepreneurs/hackers. If people want to come for a few years and move on and build something great, that's something we're proud of."[7] This statement is powerful exactly because he upended a cornerstone of how we traditionally think about talent management: that the goal of effective talent management, and effective leaders, is retention of top talent. But Zuckerberg says no, we are just as happy to have you for a defined period. Come to Facebook, he says, join us, stay as long as you like, and do something great during the time that you are here. It is a powerful, and somewhat revolutionary, statement.

How does agile talent change talent management? There are a number of ways that organizations are making this a reality.

Assess the workforce

Assessing the *true* workforce is a critical first step in rethinking talent management in the context of agile talent. The first goal is a realistic period of the organization's workforce. For example, as part of the best-in-class initiative, National City reviewed its training and development activities. In 2006, top management believed that the bank was spending $15 million for these activities, with 50 employees dedicated full-time in HR to train employees. In fact, almost 350 people were involved as internal full-time employees or external part-time people, at a total cost just short of $50 million. External talent had been excluded from prior analyses.

Identify emerging areas where capability is lacking and where agile talent can close the gap

In 2014, *Computerworld* ran a story about Google and the European Union. The first sentence read, "Europe has declared war on U.S. tech companies."[8] What is interesting is how the political attacks on Google were first experienced within Google. It initially didn't know what to make of the attacks and what to do. Wasn't a better product enough? From an agile talent perspective, it might have been useful for Google management—Larry Page, Sergey Brin, Eric Schmidt, and the rest of the management team—to ask, "As we grow in influence and dominance, what is that likely to mean in terms of new or supplementary needs for expertise?" Regardless of whether the EU concerns were justified or driven by political considerations, in retrospect Google needed to identify and engage top external expertise in government relations far earlier than it did. Doing so was important in two respects, the first of which was the ability to parry EU politics. But the second was more important: teaching both senior and operating management that political considerations were a relevant input in strategic product and service planning and needed to be part of the skill set of any Google senior executive. This lesson was not lost on Sheryl Sandberg, a former executive of Google and now chief operating officer of Facebook as she guided the implementation of Facebook's mobile strategy.

Share experience and recommendations

Some years ago, one of us (Jon) received a call from the office of Lou Noto, chairman of Mobil Oil (before its acquisition by Exxon). Noto was raised in the Bronx and was not known to mince words. As soon as he picked up the receiver, he said, "I like knowing the consultants we're using. Our number one consultant by what we spent was McKinsey. I know them. Second was Booz Allen, and I know them. Your firm is number three. Who the hell are you guys?" Noto's gruff honesty led to a good conversation then and is a very good example of the value of sharing experience.

Taking a page from the Noto playbook, we suggest that in specific technical or functional areas, management sit down and annually review the organization's experience of working with external expertise: specific individuals, teams, and firms. Using a similar process, Duke Corporate Education, the executive education arm of Duke University's Fuqua School of Business, approached a number of its guest faculty and established extended contracts for those receiving higher reviews from clients and Duke Corporate Education colleagues. This was win-win, made possible by regular review of guest faculty, saved Duke Corporate Education money, gave the faculty a fuller calendar, and ensured that top talent was deployed against Duke's demanding executive clients.

Create the role of external talent manager

As organizations make greater use of agile talent, it's important for leaders to have outside-in insight on external talent. This suggests a new role, that of chief *external* talent officer. Too often, the choice of external experts is left to "who knows whom" and is uninformed by due diligence that would share knowledge of whom the organization has worked with in past, their strengths and weaknesses, and their cultural fit. Rather than leave selection to the sole discretion of individual managers or to the purchasing department, organizations benefit by an increasing depth of knowledge of what expertise is out there, who the organization has used in the past and with what result, and who is best able to provide value in a particular capability area.

The chief external talent officer is an imagined role: we know of no organization that currently has such a role. But it is coming, and we see more green shoots all the time. For example, Jen Simpson, a managing director at Gladstone Capital, a US investment bank, describes her role this way: "Any successful financial deal maker has to be a talent manager. I can't do my job—originating and closing deals—without a deep network that we access regularly for advice, expertise and partnership. I spend a good deal of my time actively seeking out and establishing relationships with firms and individuals who could be helpful in making the deal work. That includes veterans of specific industries, debt and equity co-investors, and experts in their technical fields, such as accounting, tax, environmental, technology, and even industrial psychologists."[9]

Hold managers accountable for internal-external team effectiveness

Managers in many organizations are evaluated for their performance as team leaders. We are suggesting that, as dependence on external resources increases, performance management systems explicitly call out how well managers contribute to internal-external teamwork and productivity by setting goals and measures and then directly providing feedback related to successes or failures.

Invite externals more fully into the tent

There are good and logical reasons for limiting the involvement of external agile talent. Obviously, some information is confidential and should not be shared. Leaders might feel that employee events usually have a team-building element and that external resources are, after all, not a real part of the team; they would feel uncomfortable and employees might see them as a distraction. And there is the concern that involving external talent too deeply in employee events is an unnecessary cost ("They could be working"), that their development ought not be a concern of the client ("That's why they get the big bucks"), and that treating them as employees might send the wrong signals. It might even lead to cost, if the contractor decides to take legal action and claims he or she should have been treated as a regular employee. With all these concerns, our research strongly suggests that organizations should do more to treat externals as part of the team. Involve them in the stream of communication where at all possible. Engage them in organizational events. Give them the same permissions and discounts in the company cafeteria. Invite them to participate—and to teach—in relevant organizational events. Since agile talent will likely be more a part of how we staff the work of our organizations, we need to develop new disciplines that are inclusive rather than exclusive.

Create alumni networks, and use them to stay in touch with the bleeding edge

Companies such as P&G and McKinsey have been trailblazers in creating employee alumni networks. We propose taking the idea a step further and creating a range of internal-external alumni networks that bring people back together for learning, sharing, and expanding their relationships.

Agile Talent Changes How We Support Careers

According to a recent Freelancers Union survey, 40 million people are part of the agile talent movement in the United States. While computing is a significant work category in the study, many other industries are also represented. The survey also explodes the belief that external resources are often individuals who lost their jobs in large organizations and are unable to be resituated as employees. In fact, the Freelancers Union study points out that more than half the individuals are external by choice rather than necessity.[10]

With so large a segment of the population involved as agile talent, it's not surprising that the trend is changing how these individuals think about and develop their careers and which tools they find most helpful. The first tool is a *new concept of community*. Professional associations were created to support individual professionals and organizations in the growth of functional skills and careers. Unions arose to protect the workforce from exploitation. But times have changed, and as agile talent has become a distinct community, these professionals—particularly individual experts unaffiliated with a specific organization—have created their own organizations to provide one another support, camaraderie, and the tools of the agile-talent trade. These communities are connected and widespread: there are agile-talent-relevant associations in most European countries and North America. For example, the Freelancers Union, with 250,000 members, provides a range of networking events and skill-building opportunities in areas like how to negotiate your rates like an expert.

The second tool is *interpersonal skills*. Most organizations recruiting for full-time employment pay attention to cultural fit as well as functional skill and experience. A recent *Harvard Business Review* report points out that senior managers generally see fit as a more important determinant of success than specific technical skills.[11] Consistent with this trend, agile talent is increasingly expected to bring along the interpersonal skills and self-insight needed to effectively enter the organization, hit the ground running, and quickly build good relationships with internal staff and management. Smart leaders use a number of tools to get at cultural fit: describing the organization's culture and asking interview questions are an obvious way (e.g., "Teamwork is very important to us. What's an example of how you turned around a dysfunctional team that was not interacting well with you into a high-performance situation?"). But organizations are increasingly applying well-honed interviewing techniques such as case situations: "You find yourself in a difficult situation with your project manager. He is young, relatively inexperienced, and brimming with self-confidence—

some say arrogance. He wants to tell you how to do your work, and you are not pleased with how it's going. What do you do? Stay and suffer? Leave? Can you fix it?" Leaders also consider references from an individual's prior assignments to establish the likely cultural fit of the external expert.

The third tool is *increased movement across industries and geographic areas*. As agile talent continues to grow, a variety of organizations have started up to support this population and link external experts to project opportunities in industry. For example, Upwork is an electronic marketplace for agile talent, representing a quarter of a million businesses seeking agile talent, and eight million individuals and teams. But Upwork isn't alone. Freelancers.net provides the same service to agile talent in the United Kingdom, and organizations like Authentic Jobs focus on agile talent in specific creative fields. This infrastructure enables the development of a truly global marketplace where external talent can connect with organizations that need their skill and support on an ongoing or specific-project basis.

The fourth tool comes from *new sources of support for development*. Employees of large organizations are typically focused on how to succeed and grow within their own company or agency; the career is defined fairly specifically, and development is similarly focused on the skill needs of the organization. For agile talent, technology is offering new sources of support for professional development. These sources include better research on professional success drivers and new sources of assistance with skill building. As one example of better research, the RBL Group regularly teams up with the University of Michigan and HR associations around the world to assess the competencies expected of HR professionals. This research has been particularly helpful and relevant to external HR experts who need to operate in a wide range of HR organizations. ReSkill is a good example of skill-building assistance. This start-up combines a job site with assistance in career and skill development and provides members with skill evaluation, educational recommendations to close skill gaps, industry updates, and meet-ups that help externals build their network.

Finally, the last tool is what we call *in, out, and back in*. The Accenture careers website describes a professional who joined Accenture, left to join a client organization in search of work-life balance, and has recently been welcomed back. In fact, Accenture created a special alumni-recruiting team to focus on this population, as well as an alumni network to keep in touch with former associates. The firm is not alone. Intel is working on staying engaged with targeted high-performing employees who have left, people who were offered a job and turned it down, retirees who want to come back to work, interns who performed well but took jobs elsewhere, and so on. Basically, this group includes "the fish that got away" and people who worked well within the company at one time and would be welcomed back. The term for this approach is *boomerang hiring*. Hiring a boomerang employee has one of the highest returns on recruiting investment an employer can ask for. The cost to rehire a boomerang employee has been reported to be one-third to two-thirds the cost of hiring a "virgin" employee. Little time or effort must be invested in getting to know the candidate.

Boomerangs can be valuable to an organization because they understand the culture. They have a history with the business, or at least have been thoroughly vetted by the business, but they bring a fresh perspective from the outside. During their absence, there is a good chance that boomerangs have learned new skills and strategies, achieving success in a different setting. (If they haven't been successful, why bring them back?) They probably have made new connections and expanded their network. Organizations across industries and locations recognize that prodigals return with valuable skills and experiences that contribute to organizational capability and performance.

Getting Started: A Ninety-Day Plan

How can leaders better prepare their organizations to take advantage of agile talent? In chapter 1, we shared a framework for building effective relationships between external resources and the organizations they serve. We described four categories of alignment that were particularly important: strategic, performance, relationship, and administrative.

What are the key elements and actions of a ninety-day plan? We suggest the following steps:

- **STRATEGIC ALIGNMENT**: Have HR conduct an agile-talent audit. Key questions include these: Where are we using external resources? What are they working on? Why are we using external resources—are we doing it to supplement internal capability, to reduce cost, to obtain skills not present in the organization? Are we using our agile talent well? Are there important areas where we should be using it more or differently? Are there any areas where we should shift from internal to external resources, or from external expertise to internal staff, to better leverage our resource time and expense to address more strategic requirements?

- **PERFORMANCE ALIGNMENT**: Organize management and professional focus groups in the parts of the organization that are the chief users of agile talent. Ask questions like these: How do we assess the performance of external resources? How well do we provide feedback on strengths and weaknesses? How well do we share assessments of individuals, teams, or firms across the organization? How effective overall is our performance management of agile talent? .

- **RELATIONSHIP ALIGNMENT**: Survey the experiences of both internal and external professionals: How do agile-talent professionals describe their experience of working with our organization? How do current and recent externals describe their level of engagement? How well do we set them up for success? How well are they treated by internal staff? What is the experience of our internal staff in working together with external talent? What are we doing well? What should we start, stop, or do differently to increase collaboration?

- **ADMINISTRATIVE ALIGNMENT**: Review your administrative procedures from two perspectives—organizational need and agile-talent commitment and performance. Ask the following key questions: How does the administrative staff describe what it's like to deal with external talent—what procedures and policies work well? Which are problematic from an administrative perspective and should be changed to improve effectiveness and efficiency? How do external professionals describe their administrative interactions with the organization? What do these experts say works well, and what works less well? What are their recommendations for change?

These steps are achievable in ninety days and will give the organization insight on what can and should change. And through this overall assessment, the organization is better able to build a strategic plan to optimize effectiveness and efficiency in its overall workforce, one that combines full-time employees and agile talent. The steps required to build this plan were described in chapter 1 and are repeated in figure 9-2.

From Arrogance to Outreach in Agile Talent

The RBL Group data on our survey of thousands of managers' leadership competence suggests a final point as organizations shift from a segmented workforce strategy to a comprehensive one that

FIGURE 9-2

Making agile talent work

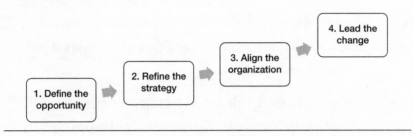

incorporates agile talent. As we saw, the human capital developer focuses on the talent required in the future as strategy shifts and as capability requirements change. Just as companies actively recruit full-time employees, we imagine a time not far from now when organizations also actively recruit external partners. What do organizations need to do and look like if they want to be positioned to attract the best agile talent from external sources?

We will probably see some or all of the following actions in the not-too-distant future:

- HR will play a significantly broader and greater role in attracting, engaging, and building relationships with high-performing agile talent and will invest more in organizations representing external resources such as the Freelancers Union in the United States, Aprotrad in France, and Ipse in the United Kingdom.

- Companies will operate with a chief external talent manager or will combine internal and external recruiting and talent management roles and will share performance information more regularly and actively.

- Organizations will invest more substantially in external-talent orientation and will even provide education and skill building to close the cultural gap where the individual's technical skills are exemplary and rare.

- Companies will measure and care about external resource engagement and take action on impediments to external performance and satisfaction.

- Organizations will experiment with different types of relationships and contracts. For example, British Gas recently signed a UK colleague to work with it on a long-term contract specifying one hundred days of work each year. The expert is not interested in a full-time career with British Gas, and the company doesn't see the value of hiring him full time when it can meet its needs (and his) on a gig basis.

- Rewards will evolve: outstanding external talent will receive "stay" and performance bonuses to ensure continuity.

It All Depends on Leadership

Finally, the effectiveness of agile talent in any organization will turn on the quality of leadership. The leadership code provides a systematic and helpful way to think about what competent leaders do. The five leadership disciplines—strategist, executor, talent manager, human capital developer, and personal proficiency—are clearly relevant to the new challenges that are posed by cloud resourcing. And among these challenges, the first is to bring the concepts of leadership up-to-date. Historically, good leadership begins and ends at the boundary of the organization. In a cloud-resourcing environment, the boundaries change and recede.

For example, consider the ten critical conditions that strategy consultant Ram Charan invites organizations to consider when they assess how well their company develops leadership for the highest levels (table 9-1).[12]

What readers might notice is that the ten conditions Charan poses all pertain to managing full-time permanent employees. In a traditional model of cloud resourcing, this outlook would work . . . maybe. But keep in mind that Accenture estimates that 20 to 30 percent of a typical big company workforce is based on agile talent. Intuit reckons the percentage could rise further by 2020. Charles Handy, back in 1989, anticipated cloud resourcing.[13] Our view of a competent leader needs to

TABLE 9-1

Critical conditions for developing leadership at the highest levels

1. Developing other leaders is an important part of every leader's job at my company. Leaders are expected to devote considerable energy and a minimum of 20 percent of their quality time to it.
2. Leaders who identify and develop other leaders are rewarded and recognized for doing so.
3. Bosses regularly coach leaders on the one or two most important things they need to improve, such as specific aspects of business acumen or relationship skills.
4. Evaluations at least once a year consider not just what the leader achieved but also how and under what circumstances the leader achieved it.
5. Leaders pool their insights to determine how a junior leader might develop and where he or she should go next.
6. The most promising leaders often get assignments that are much more challenging and may be far outside their demonstrated area of expertise.
7. Leaders on development paths aren't kept waiting for job openings. They get challenging new assignments as soon as they're ready for them or even just before.
8. Assessments of leaders' talents are precise, balanced, and complete. They are separate from annual performance appraisals.
9. Leadership development is as consistent and rigorous as processes for business items such as revenues, margins, or cash.
10. HR ensures that leaders at all levels actively develop other leaders and plan their succession. It provides useful input to help up-and-coming leaders and their bosses find good fits between people and jobs.

Source: Adapted from Ram Charan, Leaders at All Levels (San Francisco: Jossey Bass, 2008).

evolve in turn. We are excited by the ideas we have delineated in these chapters and are eager to make this more of a global conversation. We'd love to hear your stories about success and failure as you pursue a path of traditional, surgical, or transformational change in agile talent. Stay in touch with us at www.agiletalentcollaborative.com. We have posted more information and videos as a resource for your efforts.

Appendix

Your Company's Agile Talent Effectiveness Quotient (EQ)

The response to the concept of agile talent has been exciting and gratifying. We've made dozens of presentations and led many workshops with executive teams as we've developed and tested the concepts and tools. The response has been both encouraging and very helpful in building a shared methodology and framework for improvement. As one thoughtful executive put it, "None of these ideas are revolutionary, and yet, in totality, it is a revolutionary approach. I can't think of an organization I know that has put these ideas to work in managing external talent. Thank you for considerably increasing my toolkit in an area of real and increasing importance to us."

Agile Talent isn't the first book to identify the profound workforce shift that we call cloud resourcing. Whatever terms are used—the gig economy, the sharing revolution, or the freelancer movement—numerous pundits have pointed to the shift. But describing the shift is the easy part. The ability to take fuller advantage of the shift to improve organizational performance is the missing link thus far.

Our work closes the gap. It's not enough to admire the shift. Our focus is what to do about it to create opportunity and value. What specifically can organizations and their leaders do to take practical advantage of their investment in external talent? In other words, how can organizations attract the right external talent, give these individuals the right work, engage them, establish a collaborative environment, and manage and organize the work in the most productive and effective way?

A key tool to get started is what we call the *agile-talent effectiveness quotient* (EQ). This appendix introduces the EQ survey we've developed, with a taster presented here. The full version of the EQ survey is available online at our website, agiletalentcollaborative.com.

We have also taken the suggestion of HR and line executives to form a collaborative organization we call the Agile Talent Collaborative. The team has created a new venture to focus on the effective management and performance of external talent and is creating the methodology and tool kit to provide the strategic advisory services, the global database, and other tools to implement best practices and put in place the change-management skills and activities to make agile talent a sustainable source of value.

This appendix, along with the resources available on Agile Talent Collaborative (or ATC), shows how using the survey and other tools presented in *Agile Talent* can significantly increase a leadership team's understanding of how specific changes can break down the problem, improve performance, plan more effectively for change, and make more specific and targeted improvements.

How to Use the Agile Talent (EQ) Survey

The four dimensions of effective external talent management—alignment along strategic, performance, relationship, and administrative dimensions—described in chapter 1, form the basis of a brief but comprehensive survey of agile talent effectiveness.

The following questions represent a subset of the items in the more comprehensive agile talent EQ survey presented at the website agiletalentcollaborative.com. By answering these questions, you can begin to assess how effective your organization is at attracting and managing agile talent. For each item, rate your organization from 1 to 7, where 1 means "consistently inadequate," 4 means "mixed," and 7 means "consistently excellent."

1. **STRATEGIC ALIGNMENT:** How well linked is our agile-talent approach to our strategy; clear, achievable goals; the right level of sponsorship; and a realistic budget and schedule?

   _____ We use a consistent set of criteria in choosing outside partners.

   _____ We ensure that the work of external resources is based on realistic goals and time frames.

   _____ When the scope of work changes, the budget and schedule implications are addressed collaboratively.

   _____ We make sure our external resources understand the broader context and impact of the work they are doing.

2. **PERFORMANCE ALIGNMENT:** How well do we provide clear objectives, timelines, and metrics; disciplined and rigorous assessments; and useful and actionable feedback?

   _____ We encourage agile talent to communicate concerns before they become bigger problems.

   _____ We regularly evaluate the work of external resources and provide honest performance feedback.

   _____ When external resources do excellent work, we make sure to acknowledge their excellent performance.

_____ We establish clear milestones and achievement dates before teams begin their projects.

3. **RELATIONSHIP ALIGNMENT:** How well do we ensure cultural fit with our agile talent, and how good are our onboarding and orientation, engagement and involvement, and problem resolution processes?

_____ We do a good job of onboarding our agile talent to the organization's culture and way of working.

_____ We keep external resources up-to-date on what's happening in our organization, especially where their work is concerned.

_____ We actively seek feedback from our external resources on how we can improve.

_____ We consider external resources our partners, so we treat them as partners.

4. **ADMINISTRATIVE ALIGNMENT:** How well do we treat externals and handle nonbureaucratic procedures, prompt payment, and problem resolution?

_____ We ensure that external resources know our expectations, including pertinent rules and procedures before they begin work.

_____ We are tough but fair and reasonable in negotiating fees and expenses.

_____ We do not burden agile talent with unhelpful bureaucracy or excessive administrative requirements.

_____ When hiring agile talent, our decision making is reasonably prompt.

Depending on your scores on the above items, you can make some interesting observations by following these steps:

1. **ADD UP YOUR SCORES ON THE SURVEY.** The team can quickly see areas of relative strength and concern in the four areas of alignment—strategic focus, performance management, effective internal and external relationships, and administrative ease

   Figure A-1 is an example of one individual's completed survey. The chart offers immediate insight into the areas where she believes the organization is doing an excellent job of working with agile talent or where improvement is desirable or necessary. In this case, strategic alignment and administrative alignment are either mixed or better. However, relationship alignment—engaging external talent and ensuring good ongoing communication, internal staff skills, and the right orientation in working with external colleagues—is a pressure point and should be addressed. And performance alignment is also at the low end and should be examined. Does the organization have an effective, efficient, and ongoing protocol for the performance management and feedback of external talent?

2. **COMBINE INDIVIDUAL RATINGS INTO A TEAM PROFILE.** In combining ratings, you can see the overall pattern and can compare them with external talent ratings to identify areas of disagreement. As a group, the average of these ratings builds an overall perspective on perceived strengths and weaknesses. It is important to look at both overall and individual or subteam ratings to ensure a complete and accurate picture of where strengths lie and where improvement is needed. For example, working recently with an executive team, the head

FIGURE A-1

Example of agile talent effectiveness quotient (EQ) results

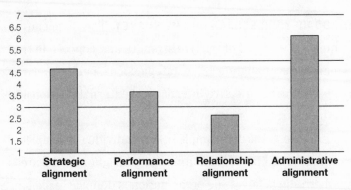

In this example, an executive used the EQ survey to rate her organization's effectiveness in managing agile talent. There were eight items per category, with a numerical rating scale of 1 to 7, where 1 = consistently inadequate, 4 = mixed, and 7 = consistently excellent. To use the same approach for a team, a manager could either add up individual ratings or average the ratings of team members.

of the business initially described a rosy view of the composite agile talent EQ. However, when all members of the leadership team had weighed in, it was clear that the organization had work to do.

3. **ASK KNOWLEDGEABLE AND VALUED EXTERNAL TALENT TO COMPLETE THE SURVEY.** In so doing, ask them to describe their experience of working with your organization. Now compare their perspective with that of the internal team. Then, compare these external ratings with the ratings of the leadership team. Use this point of comparison to identify missed areas of strength and need for improvement.

4. **IDENTIFY TWO OR THREE AREAS WHERE CHANGE IS NEEDED AND WHERE THE COST OR TIME INVOLVED IN MAKING CHANGE IS MANAGEABLE.** Using the team ratings, or combination of internal and external ratings, identify two or three areas

where change would be beneficial. There is no right or wrong in identifying needs for improvement, but we suggest that the approach focus on two dimensions: what areas will provide the best return on improvement, and where is the cost or difficulty required to change manageable. Processes like "work out" are helpful means of determining the change plan and getting key people on board for the change (see chapter 9).

5. **ESTABLISH RESPONSIBILITIES FOR MAKING THE CHANGES, DEVELOP A TIMELINE, AND PROVIDE RESOURCES IF NEEDED.** For example, can the changes be made within thirty to sixty days? Again, processes like "work out" are helpful in this step,

6. **FOLLOW UP, APPROVE THE CHANGES, AND IDENTIFY ADDITIONAL NEEDS FOR IMPROVEMENT.** Finally, ensure a rigorous approach to follow-up and approval. By setting clear and rigorous (but achievable) deadlines and utilizing a formal process of review, you are likely to achieve greater practical benefit.

For More Diagnostics and Tools

At the Agile Talent Collaborative website, you will find a large and quickly growing global database on agile talent EQ. The site also shows more generally how top companies work with external agile talent to build competitive capability and advantage. The ATC database provides leadership teams with immediate insight on the specific areas where change will lead to more effective use of agile talent. We encourage you to complete the full online survey at agiletalentcollaborative.com.

Upon completion, you will receive a comparison of your scores with global trends and will readily see where your scores are higher than the norm and potentially represent best practices, but also where your scores are well below average. Comparing the ratings of your organization's agile talent EQ with those of the hundreds of organizations in the ATC database will provide useful guidance on where change is needed in your organization.

Notes

Chapter 1

1. Sara Horowitz and Fabio Rosati, "53 Million Americans Are Freelancing, New Survey Finds," freelancersunion.org, September 9, 2014, https://www.freelancersunion.org/blog/dispatches/2014/09/04/53million/.

2. See, for example, Dave Ulrich, Jon Younger, Wayne Brockbank, and Mike Ulrich, *HR from the Outside In* (New York: McGraw Hill, 2012).

3. Lisa Disselkamp, Werner Nieuwoudt, and David Parent, "Workforce on demand," Deloitte University Press, February 27, 2015, http://dupress.com/articles/on-demand-workforce-human-capital-trends-2015/.

4. Pat Hedley, personal communication with authors, 2014.

5. Zhu Lui and Yong Geng, "Is China Producing Too Many PhDs?" *Nature*, June 2011.

6. Ulrich et al., *HR from the Outside In*.

7. Dave Ulrich, Norm Smallwood and Kate Sweetman, *The Leadership Code: Five Rules to Lead By* (Boston: Harvard Business Review Press, 2008).

8. Reid Hoffman, Ben Casnocha, and Chris Yeh, "Tours of Duty: The New Employer-Employee Compact," *Harvard Business Review*, June 2013.

9. Rob Asghar, "What Millennials Want in the Workplace (and Why You Should Start Giving It to Them)," *Forbes*, January 13, 2014.

10. Chris Osika, "Next-Generation Knowledge Workers: Accelerating the Disruption in Business Mobility," white paper, Cisco Systems, October 8, 2013, http://blogs.cisco.com/sp/next-generation-knowledge-workers-accelerating-the-disruption-in-business-mobility.

11. Bedford Group, "Client/Agency Relationship Sustainability," white paper, Bedford Group, 2014, http://bedfordgroupconsulting.com/marketing-insights/agency-relationship-sustainability/.

12. Steve Crabtree, "Worldwide, 13% of Employees Are Engaged at Work," Gallup.com, October 8, 2013, http://www.gallup.com/poll/165269/worldwide-employees-engaged-work.aspx.

13. McKinsey Global Institute, "How to Beat the Transformation Odds," *McKinsey Insights & Publications*, April 2015, www.mckinsey.com/insights/organization/how_to_beat_the_transformation_odds.

14. Hans-Henrik Jorgensen, Laurence Owen, and Andreas Neus, "Making Change Work." IBM Global Business Services, 2008.

15. Economist Intelligence Unit, "Closing the gap: The link between project management excellence and long-term success," 2009, http://www.oracle.com/oms/eppm/report-economistintelligenceunit-en-248045.pdf.

16. B. Johnson and D. Hencke, "Not Fit for Purpose: Two Billion Pound Cost of Government's IT Blunders," *Guardian*, January 5, 2008.

17. Michael Bloch, Sven Blumberg, and Jürgen Laartz, "Delivering large scale IT projects on time, on budget and on value" McKinsey & Co., October 2012, http://www.mckinsey.com/insights/business_technology/delivering_large-scale_it_projects_on_time_on_budget_and_on_value.

18. Yves L. Doz and Gary Hamel, *Alliance Advantage: The Art of Creating Value Through Partnering* (Boston: Harvard Business Review Press, 1998).

19. Kathryn Rudie Harrigan, *Managing for Joint Venture Success* (New York: Lexington, 1986).

20. Jody Freeman and Martha Minow, *Government by Contract: Outsourcing and American Democracy* (Boston: Harvard University Press, 2009).

21. See, for example, Rachel L. Swarns, "Freelancers in the 'Gig Economy' Find a Mix of Freedom and Uncertainty," *New York Times*, February 9, 2014; Sarah Kessler, "Pixel and Dime: On (Not) Getting By in the Gig Economy," *Fast Company*, May, 2014; "There's an App for That: Freelance Workers Available at a Moment's Notice Will Reshape the Nature of Companies and the Structure of Careers," *Economist*, January 3, 2015.

22. TEKsystems, "Exploring the Consultant's Overall Dissatisfaction with the IT Staffing Industry," www.teksystems.com/resources/thought-leadership/it-talent-management/exploring-consultant-dissatisfaction#section1, accessed July 27, 2015.

Chapter 2

1. Dave Ulrich and Norm Smallwood, "Capitalizing on Capabilities," *Harvard Business Review*, June 2004.

2. Ibid.

Chapter 3

1. Peter Pae, "Hedge on Fuel Prices Pays Off," *Los Angeles Times*, May 30, 2008.

2. Walter Isaacson, *Steve Jobs* (New York: Simon & Schuster, 2013).

3. KPMG, "State of the Outsourcing Industry 2013: Executive Findings," company report, April 2013, http://www.kpmg-institutes.com/content/dam/kpmg/sharedservicesoutsourcinginstitute/pdf/2013/state-of-outsourcing-2013-exec-findings-hfs.pdf.

4. James Monks, "Who Are the Part-Time Faculty?" *American Association of University Professors*, July–August 2009, www.aaup.org/article/who-are-part-time-faculty#.UzA2Ftz-a9Z.

5. Andy Young, "Geeks in Residence: Embedding Tech in the Engine Rooms of the Arts," *Guardian*, February 28, 2014, www.theguardian.com/ culture-professionals-network/culture-professionals-blog/2014/feb/28/ geeks-residence-tech-arts-developer#img-1.

6. Ibid.

7. Boris Groysberg, *Chasing Stars: The Myth of Talent and the Portability of Performance* (Princeton, NJ: Princeton University Press, 2010).

8. Robert K. Mautz and Hussein A. Sharaf, *The Philosophy of Auditing* (Madison, WI: American Accounting Association, 1961).

Chapter 4

1. Jordan Price, "Why I Just Quit My Job at Apple," *Huffington Post*, February 11, 2014, www.huffingtonpost.com/jordan-price/why-i-quit-my-job-at-apple_b_4769885.html.

2. Russ Mitchell, "How to Manage Geeks," *Fast Company*, June 1999.

3. Airbnb, "Building at Airbnb," web page, www.airbnb.com/jobs/departments/ engineering, accessed July 18, 2015.

4. Thomas O. Davenport, "The Four Stages of the Employee Value Proposition," ERE Media *TLNT, Talent Management and HR* (blog), February 20, 2013, www.eremedia.com/tlnt/the-4-stages-of-the-employee-value-proposition/.

5. Kecia Bal, "Making the Most of an EVP," *Human Resource Executive Online*, December 3, 2013, www.hreonline.com/HRE/view/story.jhtml?id= 534356471.

6. Lydia Abbott, "More Edge, Less Vanilla: 5 Hilarious Employer Branding Videos," *LinkedIn Talent Blog*, March 7, 2014, http://talent.linkedin.com/blog/index .php/2014/03/7-funny-employer-branding-videos.

7. Talya N. Bauer. "Onboarding New Employees: Maximizing Success," SHRM. org, 2010, http://www.shrm.org/about/foundation/products/Documents/Onboarding%20EPG-%20FINAL.pdf.

Chapter 5

1. Gene W. Dalton and Paul H. Thompson, *Novations: Strategies for Career Management* (Glenview, IL: Scott Foresman, 1986).

2. See Paul H. Thompson, Robin Zenger Baker, and Norman Smallwood, "Improving Professional Development by Applying the Four-Stage Career Model," *Organizational Dynamics* 15, no. 2 (Autumn 1986), 49–62; Jon Younger and Kurt Sandholtz, "Helping R&D Professionals Build Successful Careers," *Research Technology Management* 40, no. 6 (November–December 1997).

3. Tom Jones, cited in Robert N. Charette, "An Engineering Career: Only a Young Person's Game?" *IEEE Spectrum*, September 4, 2013, http://spectrum.ieee.org/ riskfactor/computing/it/an-engineering-career-only-a-young-persons-game.

4. K. Anders Ericsson, Ralf Th. Krampe and Clemens Tesch-Romer, "The Role of Deliberate Practice in the Acquisition of Expert Performance," *Psychological Review* 100, no. 3, (1993): 363–406.

5. James O'Brien, "The IT Salary 'Wave': Skills, Salaries, and the Coming Reckoning," *The Plug*, May 21, 2013, www.switchon.eaton.com/plug/article.aspx/the-it-salary-wave-skills-salaries-and-the-co.

6. Younger and Sandholtz, "Helping R&D Professionals Build Successful Careers."

7. Dalton and Thompson, *Novations: Strategies for Career Management.*

8. Adam Bryant, "Google's Quest to Build a Better Boss," *New York Times*, March 12, 2011, http://www.nytimes.com/2011/03/13/business/13hire.html.

9. Novations Group study of IBM R&D software project teams, unpublished document.

Chapter 6

1. Marcus Buckingham and Curt Coffman, *First, Break All the Rules: What the World's Greatest Managers Do Differently* (New York: Simon & Schuster, 1999); quotation from Curt Coffman, interview by Barb Sanford, *Gallup Business Journal*, June 3, 2002, www.gallup.com/businessjournal/238/building-highly-engaged-workforce.aspx.

2. Steve Crabtree, "Worldwide, 13% of Employees Are Engaged at Work," *Gallup*, October 8, 2013, http://www.gallup.com/poll/165269/worldwide-employees-engaged-work.aspx.

3. In early versions of the VOI^2C^2E model, the "empowerment" factor was called "experimentation." The logic is similar.

4. Avi Dan, "Getting to the Bottom of What Clients Think of Agencies," *Forbes*, October 8, 2012, www.forbes.com/sites/avidan/2012/10/08/getting-to-the-bottom-of-what-clients-think-of-agencies/2/.

5. All quotes in this section are from ibid.

6. Gordon Perchthold and Jenny Sutton, "How to Lead Consultants to Exceed Expectations," *Ivey Business Journal* (September–October 2010), http://iveybusinessjournal.com/publication/how-to-lead-consultants-to-exceed-expectations/.

7. J. Richard Hackman and Greg R. Oldham, *The Job Diagnostic Survey: An Instrument for the Diagnosis of Jobs and Evaluation of Job Redesign Projects* (Arlington, VA: Office of Naval Research, 1974).

8. Jon R. Katzenbach and Douglas K. Smith, *The Wisdom of Teams: Creating the High-Performance Organization* (Boston: Harvard Business Review Press, 1992).

9. Ben Horowitz, "Good Product Manager, Bad Product Manager," unpublished memo, 1996, text available at http://a16z.com/2012/06/15/good-product-managerbad-product-manager/.

Chapter 7

1. Dave Ulrich, Norm Smallwood, and Kate Sweetman, *The Leadership Code: Five Rules to Lead By* (Boston: Harvard Business Review Press, 2008).

2. See the video "Steve Jobs and The Beatles" at "Steve Jobs, 1955–2011" *60 Minutes Overtime*, October 10, 2011, http://www.cbsnews.com/news/steve-jobs-1955-2011/.

3. George Beahm, ed., *The Boy Billionaire: Mark Zuckerberg in His Own Words* (Chicago: B2 Books, 2012), 99–100.

4. RBL research note, undated.

5. Ulrich, Smallwood, and Sweetman, *The Leadership Code.*

6. Crabtree, "Worldwide, 13% of Employees Are Engaged at Work."

Chapter 8

1. This chapter benefits from the ideas in Dave Ulrich, Dale Lake, Jon Younger, and Wayne Brockbank, "Change Insights and HR Implications," *Indian NHRD Network Journal* (July 2012).

2. "Consulting Business Trends Analysis," Plunkett Research blog, November 11, 2014, www.plunkettresearch.com/trends-analysis/consulting-management-business-market/.

3. Ibid.

4. "An Interview with Dan Reardon, Chief Executive Officer, North Highland," *Leader Magazine*, November/December 2013, http://www.leadersmag.com/issues/2013.4_Oct/ROB/LEADERS-Dan-Reardon-North-Highland.html.

5. Michael Lewis, *Flash Boys: A Wall Street Revolt* (New York: Norton, 2014).

6. Asmus Komm et al., "Return on Leadership: Competencies That Generate Growth," report by Egon Zehnder International and McKinsey & Company, February 2011, www.egonzehnder.com/files/return_on_leadership_1.pdf.

7. John P. Kotter, *Leading Change* (Boston: Harvard Business Review Press, 2012).

8. Ibid.

9. *Jurassic Park*, directed by Steven Spielberg, released June 1993.

10. Jim Johnson, Karen D. Boucher, Kyle Connors, and James Robinson, "Collaborating on Project Success," Standish Group report, *Software Magazine*, February–March 2001.

11. Jerry B. Harvey, *The Abilene Paradox and Other Meditations on Management* (San Francisco: Jossey-Bass, 1996).

12. Ibid.

Chapter 9

1. Saul D. Alinsky, *Rules for Radicals* (New York: Knopf, 2010).

2. Charles Handy, *The Age of Unreason* (Boston: Harvard Business School Press, 1990). See also Lee Tom Perry, Randall G. Stott, and Norm Smallwood, *Real-Time Strategy* (New York: Wiley, 1993).

3. Anthony Ha, "Design Firm Adaptive Path Acquired by Capital One," *Tech Crunch*, October 2014.

4. Brian Hindo, "The Empire Strikes at Silos," *Businessweek*, August 19, 2007, www.bloomberg.com/bw/stories/2007-08-19/the-empire-strikes-at-silos.

5. Julia Preston, "Pinks Slips at Disney: But First, Train Foreign Replacements," *New York Times*, June 3, 2015, http://www.nytimes.com/2015/06/04/us/last-task-after-layoff-at-disney-train-foreign-replacements.html?_r=0.

6. Shelley Seifert, interview with Jon Younger, New York, 2014.

7. Beahm, ed., *The Boy Billionaire*, 99–100.

8. Preston Gralla, "Europe Has a Love/Hate Thing for U.S. Tech," *Computerworld*, September 2014.

9. Jennifer Simpson, personal correspondence with authors, 2015.

10. Horowitz Rosati, "53 Million Americans Are Freelancing."

11. Jean Martin, "For Senior Leaders, Fit Matters More Than Skill," hbr.org, January 14, 2014, https://hbr.org/2014/01/for-senior-leaders-fit-matters-more-than-skill.

12. Ram Charan, *Leaders at All Levels* (San Francisco: Jossey Bass, 2008).

13. David Gartside, Yaarit Silverstone, Catherine Farley, and Susan M. Cantrell, "The Rise of the Extended Workforce," Accenture Institute for High Performance, 2013, https://www.accenture.com/us-en/insight-future-of-hr-rise-extended-workforce.aspx; Jeff Schwartz, Josh Bersin, and Bill Pelster, "Global Human Capital Trends 2014," Deloitte University Press, 2014, http://dupress.com/periodical/trends/global-human-capital-trends-2014/?icid=hp:ft:01; Charles Handy, *The Age of Unreason* (Boston: Harvard Business School Press, 1990).

Index

Acknowledgments

Agile Talent has been a year in the writing, and another year in preparation. We have many colleagues to thank for clearing the path we have walked in completing this book. A few deserve particular mention. First, Dave Ulrich, our friend and partner at The RBL Group, has greatly informed our thinking. Second, we thank Julie Person and Jorge Figueredo of McKesson, who, by requesting a review of emerging trends in strategic HR, led us to the topic of this book. Third, we thank Martin Waters, President of the International Division of Victoria's Secret and Bath & Body Works, who became a supporter and early adopter of our work.

In addition to these individuals, we are grateful to many others: Paul Thompson and Gene Dalton for the career stages; Brook Derr for career orientations; David Maister's writings on trusted professional relationships; and Rita McGrath's work on dynamic organizational capability. In addition, we thank Aaron Younger, formerly of PwC, and Spencer Patterson, of Utah Valley University, who are our partners and cofounders of the Agile Talent Collaborative and have made significant contributions to the practical application of our work.

Many other colleagues have taught us, sparred with us, and provided helpful guidance and criticism as we've developed and tested our ideas: Telma Viale, Seamus and Helen McCardle, Jen Simpson, Bill Allen, Ron Schneiderman, Jens Jenssen, Hilde Sannes, Paul Kadin, Geeta Durham, Suzanne Pedersen, Even Bolstad, Shelley Seifert, Pat Hedley, Frank Cespedes, Soren Isaksen, Dixon Thayer, Josh Younger,

Megan Wall-Wolff, and Gabor Varjasi. We also acknowledge RBL colleagues, notably Christine Cleemann, Ernesto Uscher, Martha Liliana Ruiz, Mark Nyman, Joe Hanson, Adam Rampton, Darryl Wee, Jessica Johnson, Nate Thompson, Allan Freed, Erin Burns, Michael Phillips, Jade White, Joe Grochowski, Jayne Pauga, Justin Allen, and Lisa Griep.

A special thanks goes to Melinda Merino, our editor at Harvard Business Review Press. Melinda is a delightful, wise, and exacting editor, and it was our privilege to work with and learn from her: her nine-page, single-spaced critique of our first draft was a revelation. She is a legend in the trade, and we can't thank her enough. We also sincerely applaud Melinda's supporting team at the Press for their hard work and evident professionalism at every step in the publication of *Agile Talent*.

Finally, we dedicate this book to our dear life partners, Carolyn Younger and Tricia Smallwood, the real talent in our families.

—Jon Younger and Norm Smallwood

About the Authors

JON YOUNGER is managing partner of the Agile Talent Collaborative and partner emeritus of the RBL Group, where he led the firm's Strategic HR practice. He is a member of the executive education faculties of the Ross School of Business, University of Michigan, and the Indian School of Business in Hyderabad. Previously he was corporate senior vice president and chief learning and talent officer of a leading financial services organization. He has also served on both government and corporate boards including the Government of Singapore advisory board in HR Transformation. Jon teaches and consults with select clients in North America, Europe, and Asia who are experimenting with ways to increase the productivity and engagement of agile talent professionals. He is also an adviser to SRI Executive, a Dublin-based firm specializing in executive recruiting, learning, and organizational development, primarily in the public sector. He is a coauthor of many articles and four other books: *HR from the Outside In*, *HR Transformation*, *HR Competencies*, and *Global HR Competencies*.

NORM SMALLWOOD is cofounder of the RBL Group and is a partner with the Agile Talent Collaborative. He was a cofounder of Novations Group, a human resource services firm. Before that Norm served as an organizational development professional with Procter & Gamble and an organizational effectiveness adviser with Esso Resources Canada. He has been cited by *Leadership Excellence* as a preeminent voice in the field of leadership. He teaches and consults widely in North America, the Middle East, Latin America, and Asia. He is a coauthor of seven other books: *Real-Time Strategy*, *Results-Based Leadership*, *How Leaders Build Value*, *The Change Champion's Field Guide*, *Leadership Brand*, *Leadership Code*, and *Leadership Sustainability*.